A Box of Chocolates

Poetry &
Short Stories

Don Kahrmann

A Box of Chocolates

Indie Crawlers books may be ordered through booksellers or by contacting:

Indie Crawlers
SpiderBooksPublishing.com
(239) 693-DRAW (3729)

ISBN: 978-1-942728-32-0 (Print)
ISBN: 978-1-942728-33-7 (Digital)

Printed in the United States of America

Editor: Don Kahrman
Cover concept: Don Kahrmann
Cover & Book layout: Jennifer FitzGerald - MotherSpider.com

DARE TO BEGIN

YOU NEVER KNOW

WHAT

WILL HAPPEN

CONTENTS

SECRETARY

Judy Howell

Judy Howell is an extraordinary lady with the patience of Job. Extensive mind reading skills and remarkable ingenuity at decoding my cut and paste manuscripts. She deserves a metal.

Thank you,
thank you,
thank you!!

A BOX OF CHOCOLATES

You never know what you are going to get in this Box of Chocolates. I lived it year by year. The order, places, moments, sequences.

I planned as you planned. Feared as you feared, hurt as you hurt, struggled as you struggled, fought as you fought - for here and now.

Would I do it again? Yes. Would I change things? Yes. Regrets - several, but I did it my way like you did it your way.

Results: good, bad, indifferent. When I was forty-five I had some perspective. Now at ninety I have some understanding.

Would I change life's hourglass, of course I would. That would be never - never land. We can't go there.

Don Kahrmann
August, 2016

"We cannot direct the wind...
But we can adjust the sails."

Anonymous

DEDICATION

To

Joan Zausmer Kahrmann

who

from the beginning

gave

me support

who

shoved when I needed shoving

who

breathed fire when I needed fire

helped me do what she knew I could do.

gratefully

with love

A

Allow your door to always stand ajar.

A wind can cause a wild sea. Stand still and wait.

An ordinary moment can be very significant if you know it.

A lie often comes home to roost.

A person's smile is a reflection of that moment.

A stillness that drills into a cliff.

A sea rising and falling, rising and falling should tell you something.

At that moment I dropped into the slot I had been seeking, it exceeded what I had expected.

Appreciate today – It makes tomorrow better.

A tree trunk is a safe home for curious creatures, but who wants to live in a trunk? Spread out. Use the whole tree!

Accept the challenges. They make you who you are.

Always do your homework. Preparation!

ALONE

Let me go into my garden
it is
incurably luring
nearer
than I had remembered.

Smells tethered return to me
in other places
and bring a half forgotten second.
A butterfly
hopscotched from pink to purple.

Alone is never alone.
It is a place
I go to that is mine only.
Sit look feel –
hopelessly contented.

A WORLD BY ITSELF

Love begins in a quiet moment
given purely it grows, hungers
an ocean flowing, ebbing moving
rushing, constant – but not necessarily.

One needs levels of skills
to nurture, develop, understand
to speak or be silent
to sing out softly.

New love is not knowledge of
what one reads, sees, imagines –
it is an incendiary moment
blind of anything but feeling.

When we feel needed, cherished
know tender devotion –
it is not a fancy
but feelings strong as quick pain.

A WORLD BY ITSELF

Love can be rough edged
or delicate as dawn –
hover near the rainbow's edge
fly at you like a hatchet.

It does not come with instructions
the middle of your world
it is what it is
new petals on the wind.

Love slammed my heart
left a bruise, departed –
no objective logic
softened the slap of no.

That world turns
moves, twists, askew –
harbors memories of new beginnings
the way it always does.

AGAIN

We always say
you know what you're going to do –
– but do you

We always say
if I do this that will happen –
– happenings are slow and dissipate.

We always say
if I have to do it again I will vanish –
no, you get thinner, wiser.

We always say
if I ignore it, it will diminish –
Why can't you just be and let things alone.

We always say
I got through yesterday and today –
tomorrow will come along.

We always say
responsibility is thrust upon us –
difficult, necessary –again

We always say

A CONSPICUOUS LUNCH

It was a dog day of summer, breezeless, heavy and flat as we entered the cool, softly lighted restaurant, P.F. Chang in the Gulf Coast Town Center, Ft Myers, Florida. The interior was beautiful. There was an elaborate mural and two huge oriental lanterns suspended from the ceiling. Copies of the terra cotta soldiers from Xian, China are scattered about the room. In front of the restaurant is an enormous concrete Emperor's stallion.

The first thing we did when seated for lunch was to look at the exquisite, huge, powerful and commanding Chinese mural of Mongolian Tartars on horse back. As we adjusted our eyes to the dimly lit restaurant three things happened simultaneously. A glass crashed to the floor a long distance away, our waitress arrived immediately followed by a lady and her three children about five, seven, and ten years old who were seated at a table in front of our elevated booth.

The mother was fair, with short curly hair, arched eyebrows, medium height, nice figure. Her dress was white with an unusual gold, white and navy blue pin on one shoulder. All accessories were navy.

Her ten year old son was a carbon copy of his mother in height, weight and coloring. Even his hair was curly. A shirt was tucked into his jeans at the waist, clean sneakers and combed wavy hair.

Five year old boys are about the same – scruffy. His shirt

was out, tennis shoes untied, chubby, tanned, crew cut and a loud whiny voice.

At seven years old he was like his father, tall, olive complexion, thick dark hair, large brown eyes and graceful. Even at his age he was distinctly his own person, mature and confident.

Our waitress was thin, thick shoulder length hair and pretty. She had a bright personality and she was knowledgeable about her job.

"Welcome to P.F. Chang. What would you like to drink?" She said as she handed us the menus. "Water, tea, ice?"

She left. The family in front of us are looking at menus when the ten year old boy took the five year old brother to the toilet, who protested loudly.

Our waitress returned with our beverages and took our orders.

"Anything else?" she asked.

"Yes," I said, "do you know anything about the mural?"

"Two artists painted it. They painted a different mural in each of P.F. Chang 150 restaurants. I'll put your orders in." she answered.

Our spring rolls arrived and the table opposite us also had food.

"Could you tell us about the mural?" I asked the waitress.

"The mural shows a wealthy nobleman and Prince Khitan himself. On the far left, another unknown nobleman balances an arrow with a quiver hanging at his side. The sturdy Mongolian horse stands bridled and saddled."

We ate our food, chatted and watched the family

opposite us. Things went smoothly until the ten year old boy attempted to eat fried rice with chopsticks. He decorated the table and his mother with brown dots. The children laughed. Mother glared, our waitress returned with our egg drop soup.

"Could we have chapter two now?" I asked.

"The scene on the right of the mural shows a bridge with riders in movement. Ahead of a richly dressed mounted nobleman is Prince Khitan in an elaborate robe of Chinese silk." Smiling, she disappeared.

Suddenly the cover on a straw sailed across a lady's shoulder. It landed in a man's soup. The seven year old saw his brother's straw cover sail past his nose and walloped him good. Mother, who was pouring tea, saw nothing, but the five year old was crying loudly and he wacked his brother with his spoon. Bedlam.

Our beef and shrimp lunch bowls arrived, delicious. We ate, drank our tea, did not want dessert and asked for our check.

We were about finished when a waiter carrying an elevated tray with two glasses of water and a selection of oriental condiments, tripped. The mother and five year old child received a frontal bath. Immediately, three waiters appeared. One wiped the table, one wiped the floor and the third wiped the lady's chest.

Our waitress placed the check on our table.

"Thank you very much. Hope you enjoyed the entertainment," she said.

"Hilarious," I answered.

"One more thing about the mural. If you look closely,

you'll find the muralist paid tribute to Florida state's mocking bird. There is a hidden rabbit too."

I have trouble with my balance. After we left our booth, I started to move rapidly to my right. In reaching out to steady myself I put one hand on a man's left shoulder and my other hand in his soup.

ALICE

A Spoke In The Wheel

Alice was born on Oklahoma Territory. Her first friend was an American Indian. My first memory of Alice was watching her show my kindergarten class how to plant a tiny rose bush.

My second memory of Alice was going down the wide six inch high iron steps that was the recess entrance/exit for the kindergarten/first grade classes to the playground. I was in line following her. She was my first grade teacher. I was immature and not interested in learning to read or write. Two years with Alice was a gift. Being an only child with limited neighborhood children to play with, I was not adept at social skills. She taught me the three "R's" and information needed to function in a child's world. Six years later, I attended her wedding to my uncle - Dad's brother. She lived next door to me after that. My real education began. Alice was the most astute person I ever knew.

She was a soft blonde Scot of medium height and weight. Her nose was sharp, bordering on severe, which suited her angled features. Her hair was not styled, but cut to suit her head and face. However, her strong blue eyes were remarkable - looked directly at you which sometimes included looking through you. Sometimes I felt naked. I wondered if other people had that experience. Alice's eyes saw all - the good, bad, kind, or unkind. Her family was her children.

When Alice married my uncle I was twelve years old. My mother's slowly growing mental problems erupted into a full blown nightmare. Alice and I got home from school at the same time. We visited weekdays in her kitchen. Cookies and milk and my sanity. She explained sex. She told me some people should not marry each other. My parents were complete opposites. Alice gave me perspective in a very emotionally difficult situation. She explained I was not responsible for my Mom's mental problems nor for my family problems These problems were theirs not mine.

Whatever I told Alice was alright - whatever I said was alright. Alice sorted through the problems. We talked out whatever needed talking out, letting others slip away. If they were important they would resurface. Alice explained when I was thirteen to change what I can and accept what I could not change. Those sentences pushed the smoke away.

My friend, benefactor, confidant, straight from heaven surrogate mom was Alice. She saved me from disaster. Only the two of us knew that. The string of her story is love --Alice's love for people - for truth - for fairness - for kindness and generosity. My mother was in no condition to cope with my growing up problems, insecurities or my emotional roller coaster. My dad couldn't cope with my mom's mental illness. He lived in his own small departmentalized world. Work, movies, family, sleep.

Alice's home was much more my home than my own. Alice was there for me. All I had to do was open her side door.

A loving, secure, contented house welcomed and protected me at any age.

Alice listened carefully to every word I said. Many years later I realized how brilliant she was.

Alice's warmth, kindness and charm were freely given to everyone. I loved her unconditionally. She altered many lives. She taught by doing, slowly – large traditional celebrations, small impromptu parties with always something to make or do. Homemade Easter paper bunnies. Pin the feather on the turkey, ears on the rabbit mobile, snowflakes for the first snow. Beach wiener roasts, impromptu picnics, real fall leaf hats, spring flowers cut from magazines were glued to colored paper plates. Alice created a happy full life filled with love for her family, for her husbands, and for me. I was a spoke in the wheel.

The Point Pleasant beach house on the board walk was a huge plus for all of us in Alice's family. The house was large, old, simple with a front cement deck. Adirondack chairs, two outside rear showers – one on each side of the house and a fireplace. There was one bath down and one up. Through the years this house celebrated birthdays, anniversaries, honeymoons, christenings and funerals with laughter, love and tears.

I spent my first honeymoon there, grieved for my mother when she died, and for my marriage as it disintegrated.

Then I met a night club entertainer who dazzled me. We fell in love though miles apart in every possible way.

"Do you love her?" Alice asked me. "Yes,"

"Does she love you?"

"Yes"

"Sometimes love is not enough. She may break your heart. Are you sure? Is she the most important person in your life?"

Alice took my face in her hands as she looked at me somewhere between doubt and wisdom.

"Don, you're thirty-six years old. You've been through a war, a seven year marriage, and heartbreak with your Mother's mental illness that your father handled poorly. As your aunt and friend, I love you dearly. I saw what you went through when you were only 13 years old. You carried that cross until you went to war. That great change in your life probably saved your mind. You had your own problems which you could handle on a one to one basis. At home you couldn't solve the problems you had no control over. You're doing well now. Don't take on problems in a new marriage that you have no control over."

Unfortunately, Alice was right. My heart was broken.

Alice was married twice, widowed twice, and had a lover for the last eight years of her life. All were fine men who gave her what she deserved - love and themselves.

Dependable, steadfast, reliable - a rock I could depend upon. All of her family could. I was an outsider. She treated me like apple pie. Alice - unique, original, special. She wore an upside down lampshade at a party with witty sayings written on it. Another party featured a large skirt filled with balloons. She was a bottle of Scotch once and never wore panties. No one asked for a reason.

The military was good for me. It gave me a rest from my life. No thinking, planning, consequences or disappointments. Do what you're told. Fulfill your duties and just be. Alice's letters gave me clear perspective about my goals and future. I was in R & R but I didn't know it.

During W.W. II letters from Alice informed me about my parents and my grandmother who took care of my Mother.

She said you have a new life, new friends, plan a new future and never live at home again. The G.I. Bill provided many things in many ways.

Our relationship of Alice/mom and Don/son mellowed through all the years. We had a deep love for each other.

We simply understood. Alice was a no-nonsense woman. She stepped up to the plate bat in hand and took a strong swing. What will I do when she is gone? What she taught me. Step into the ball and swing hard.

The last I saw Alice she was seventy-five and had suffered a stroke. She couldn't walk but she understood, used one arm, and spoke slowly. Her hospital bed was in the corner of the dining room. You could see into the living room and kitchen. Retson, Alice's lover, was a gem. He knew what to do, to say, to be there for what was needed. I used to go see Alice and give him time alone. Nurses cared for her 24-7. Alice's reading ability was impaired and she wasn't happy with this condition. Three times a week I would teach her the A.B.C.'s of reading, as she taught them to me when I was six years old. I kissed her parchment cheek while holding her arthritic fingers next to mountains of veins, wrinkled skin, and furrowed knuckles. Each day I knew I might never see her alive again.

A class was ending. Alice was graduating. She had stuffed stomachs, heads and hearts. She had washed invalids, windows, minds and floors; bandaged hundreds of knees and fingers.

Walking through life Alice touched people setting their fames straight. Her hands had moved around, holding this, settling that, aiming balls, swinging bats, tending lives, planting rose bushes, fixing covers over apple pie and children asleep on the floor.

Alice loved roses. She planted them when my mom was so ill. I remember the sun on our backs as she taught me how to plant a tiny rose bush and test the soil where the plant was green.

For thirty years scarlet climbers were on a trellis, primroses next to a pole in her yard. If the earth needed fixing she fixed it - as she fixed life situations.

She now has gone to test the soil. I still step up to the plate and swing hard.

ANN

Ann was the only free spirit I ever knew. While I was in the Navy in 1945 my dad bought the shell of a house across from Ann's home. It was all finished on the outside, unfinished on the inside.

We moved into that house in late November 1946.

In January, 1947 a snowstorm surprised us and I met Ann Underwood. She was fourteen -pulling her younger sister, Dotty, on a Flexible Flyer sled.

My navy friend Guy was visiting me from Washington, D.C. We all made a large snowman and threw snowballs at each other. I remember that day clearly.

Ann was unique, always her own person. She was tall, long hair, dark eyes that saw everything kindly. I never saw her angry.

We both went to teacher's college and married when Ann was still in college. She honed her teaching skills, designed her own clothes and sewed them on a used sewing machine on our kitchen table.

She charmed students, parents, principals and me with her special brand of living. Ann was always exploring, investigating, growing and giving.

By a strange quirk of fate we were offered a job at a school in Cartagena, Columbia, South America operated by an American oil company. I was the principal of a K-8th grade school. Ann was the third grade teacher.

We received a rent free furnished five room house on the Caribbean ocean. We paid for a maid, cook, yard boy, sewing lady, and household food. We never questioned the food bill.

The population of Cartagena was very rich or very poor. Maids were poor. Ann told our maid to give each person who worked for us a hardy lunch. What our maid took home each night to help feed her family was never questioned.

About one weekend in five we took a two hour flight from Cartagena to Bogota, Cali or Medellin This was 1958-1959.

There were no roads or trains from Cartagena to the capitol. In 2009 a cruise ship stopped in Cartagena, Columbia, South America. Still no roads or trains from the coast to Bogota!

Ann loved this new free world and all our adventures.

We lived there three years. Each year we returned to New Jersey to visit our families. On our return to Columbia we visited Central American countries.

Good travelers are born, not made. Ann was an excellent traveler, never lost her cool. She charmed all she met whether she could speak their language or not.

Our interests, attitudes and points of view slowly changed. We no longer loved each other. We divorced and remained intimate friends for the next forty years.

Ann always gave me love, kindness and understanding. Most important she gave me a positive point of view which I did not understand for many years.

She moved to California and two years later married a college professor. They had two children that I watched grow up. Ann's free spirit has gone to another place.

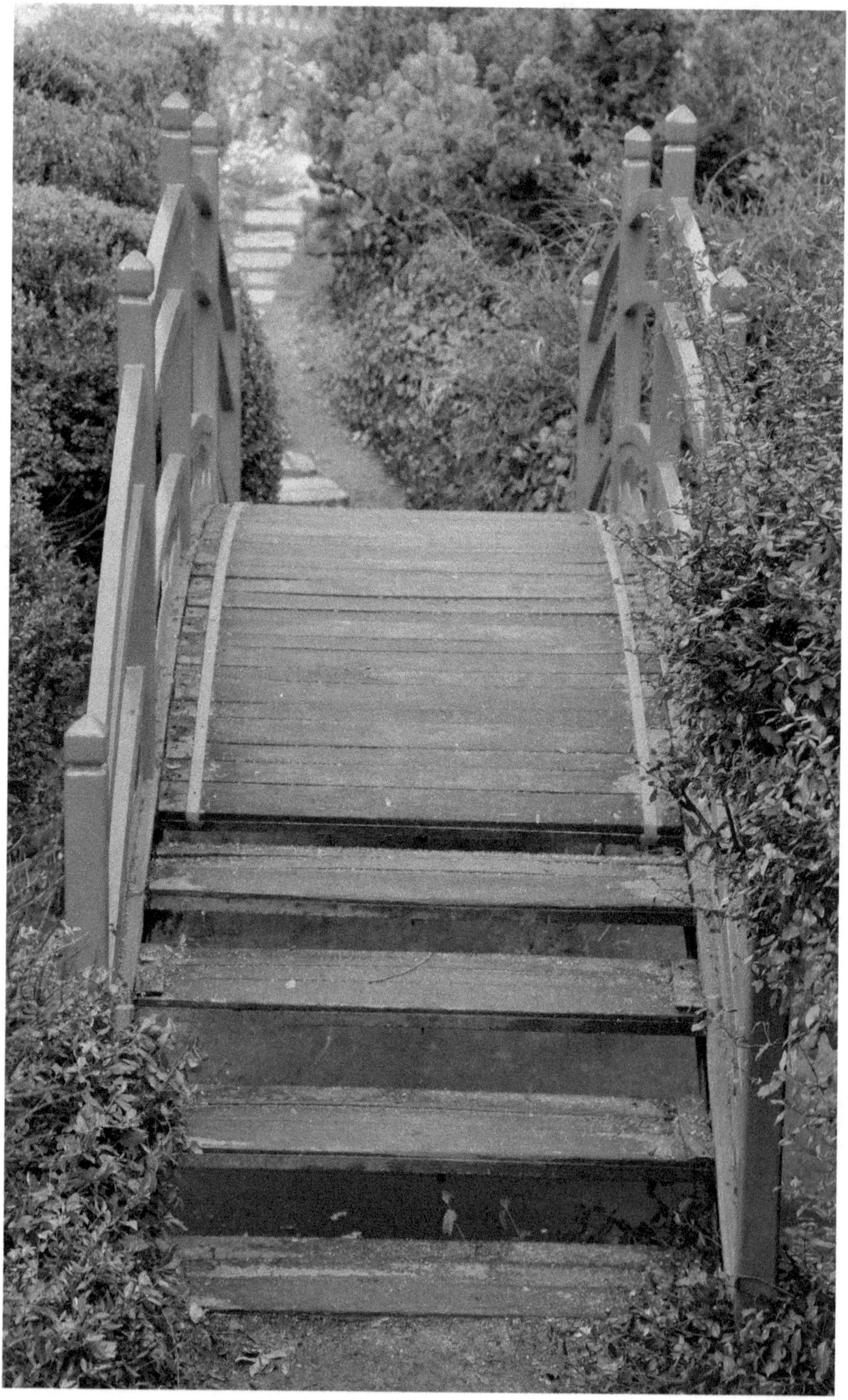

A FIFTY PERCENT LUNCH

1995

It was an ordinary lunch at I.H.O.P. before a movie. We waited a long time for the waitress to take our order. We wanted one water and one decaf. The coffee pot arrived with a cup. I poured my coffee. When I picked up the cup, the handle was cool. A new cup arrived. I poured coffee into this cup. Coffee was lukewarm. I explained to the waitress about the coffee temperature. She said she would brew a new pot.

Our food eventually arrived. It was cold - sent it back. Warmer food arrived - but not hot food. The coffee never arrived until I waved my cup like a flag at the Indy 500.

I expected the check. Had to ask for it. Finally check arrived. We had a fifty percent lunch so I left a fifty percent tip, 10% of $22.40 or $2.24.

ALWAYS THERE

His finger moved across my life and many others .

We met in Florida at the Parkway on the Caloosahatchee River in North Fort Myers in 1988. We were friends from that day forward.

Al drove a school bus, went to the army, college, marriage to Fredda for 64 years - two children. He built his own first house, worked for Sherwin Williams Paint Company for forty years and retired.

Our early lives were both tethered - his on a farm shoveling shit, driving tractors - mine, the demands of a mentally ill mother and a broken family.

He was cantankerous, stubborn, kind and generous, I am introspective, cautious, and selective. Al had an instant temper that came and went rapidly. I am self-contained, introspective and controlled.

We were both Taurus - two days apart- but so different in attitudes, temperament and desires. He liked to be patted. When he needed, I patted. Adventure, my garden and words on paper patted me.

We drove on vacation trips with Fredda and AL Everything was good, fine, fun - but we were not peas in a pod. River and Gulf of Mexico boat journeys to restaurants for lunch were adventures. Al loved his boat. He was good on the water. Life has impediments and rough winds. Al knew you headed into the wind.

He liked privacy, but was not private. He never dwelled in a world of mights, perhaps, or ifs. He lived in here, now and I will. He spoke in short sentences from point "A" to point "B". Never frivolous with words or with life. Al never pulled on a brittle wishbone.

I always liked his conversations - southern funny dry and he never knew it.

I always knew what he was about because he always knew.

If you are satisfied with your own decisions, your own performances, you are satisfied with your life. Al's performance as a husband and Fredda's as a wife, their parenting-were on the mark, true, definitive. Marriage is a tough business in the long run of things. When you do it right what an accomplishment!

Al was his own entrepreneur. He bought a 44 unit apartment complex in Greensboro, N.C., a condo in Myrtle Beach, S.C., and in Fort Myers, Fla. He owned four cars, a 32 foot boat, joined country clubs, golfed, traveled the U.S. and Europe. He liked to sit in the shade under the Fort Myers Beach pier and read. We were comfortable with each other. We were alike and not. We both had lines you couldn't cross and we never ventured over that line. Not even once.

When Al crosses my path today I talk to him and tell him why he came to mind. I think he likes that. I would.

B

Blowing pebbles along a windy mountain road.
Will they blow right or left?

Buy one, get one free! It should apply to cars, diamonds and movies.

Be happy -it gets you anonymous benefits.

Bliss is what you make it.

Begin anywhere. But begin.

Be of good faith.
It drives your enemies crazy.

Being negative requires the same energy as being positive.

Be self confident but never vain.

If you break it -fix it.

Bravery and courage are roommates.

BALLOONS

At seven a.m. in September, 2015 Joan and I walked across the grass at the Albuquerque, New Mexico Balloon Festival. Seven balloons were inflated and stood in a line ready to launch. Such activity!

Gorgeous blue sky, whispering breeze, many balloon shapes lay on the grass around us, flat, shapes of wrinkled colors. Seven balloons were up and away very rapidly. Many balloons waiting to breath, Joan smiled.

A large shiny black truck arrived with five passengers, pulling an open flat bed containing a gondola and folded balloon. Rapidly they unloaded. Two men raised the open end of the balloon while a lady pointed a large electric fan into the balloons mouth. The balloon filled rapidly as ropes were attached to the balloon and wicker gondola.

About every twenty minutes six or seven balloons ascended five minutes apart in various areas of the field.

The launchings caught you up and drew you into the action. I was in every gondola I saw launched. Few tourists spoke. We were enthralled.

Balloons floated on a blue sky with acres of ordinary grass sprinkled with dandelions and a few trembling violets.

There were two or three hundred balloons up. Dozens of buses, acres of cars parked in various designated areas, twenty-two nations were represented. Fifteen to twenty thousand people from everywhere. Crowds moved, balloons bobbed, enthusiasm floated from eyes, lips, fingers.

A glimpse of make-believe, a journey to never never land part of the twilight zone but on this side. Splashes of colors, shapes, delights. I took Joan's hand.

Our senses were overwhelmed. Movement, noise, textures, touch, wicker, ropes - joy happiness and laughter. So much pleasure on so many faces. Pure seduction! Balloon shapes close above your head. A doll, dog, flower, ball, rabbit, clown- endless joy.

We meandered among various shapes, crews and observers.

Among the visitors was a father carrying a two year old boy who was not too impressed. Perhaps it was a bit over-whelming. but the four year old daughter was enthralled.

"Daddy, it's magic!!"

She pulled on his pant's leg and pointed a finger.

We were all about her age.

BUTTERFLY

It was not yours
yesterday I spied it
black yellow orange white
resting on a short breeze

Today I spied your brother
or cousin's cousin
among softly perfumed shapes
butterfly stems that waved

Are you dead or fled
no mourning on the field breeze
but memories of dazzling rhythms
flutter in my mind

Perhaps you are a pleasure for a breeze
you twinkle past me
remembering another world
from a ballooning view

I

No one will morn you
thinning grass shadowed in sun
the world did not shut down
when you silently left

Flitting breeze captured butterflies
dizzied me with wonder
silent quiet colors mingled
in leaf shadows for a blink

In the colors of September
a folded wing
found among withered things
cracked dusty faded leaves

You are dead with your friends
I remember that glimpse of colors
that came softly on a wave
leaving me breathless

2

BARTER

Compelled by needs
stronger than fear
to engage in moments
of pretend ecstasy

deep in dim shadows
on cold streets
flashing perfect teeth
entice prey with the scent

of cheap cologne, attempting
to barter sex along with
bits of his soul
for dirty wrinkled bills

BILLIE HOLIDAY

Lady of The Camellias

A class by herself-
unique, exquisite notes
that new the bad
the ugly and the beautiful.

Her voice never wavered
she could deliver a
melody from her heart
to your heart, softly.

Drugs, whiskey, love, torment
spokes of a splintered life.
Time flipped or flopped,
no hand on the rudder.

The warp and weft
that wove the pattern was
never designed, straight,
balanced, evenly tight.

The lady of the camellias
always did it her way –
good or bad, right or wrong,
come in heartache, sit down.

BOUGAINVILLEA

Soft

delicate

alluring

hot pink, velvet purple

flowers

on

beautifully deceptive

bushes

that draw blood

BRANCH

Dry wooden branch on a tree
broken by a gentle breeze
trampled by a hoof
to replenish earth
nature grows a new tree
over there
in a dirt cradle
straddling rock boundaries
wet by ribbons of rain
finger of lightening
vulgar quiet
fried nest of eggs
burned flying squirrels
a branch of a tree
not carved for a toy
or a sling shot
condemned
to nothing

C

Children without laughter is like a brook without sounds.

Coolness -the sound of a bell as it leaves the room.

Children playing in mud are wonderful as long
as they are not your children.

Calmness should be a part of your day.
Be sure to find some.

Calamity happens often. Be prepared mentally.

Cleanliness is not next to Godliness, it is next to
whomever you are sitting next to.

Calm is within, never without.

Contents of anything is only the beginning.

Collect friends but be particular.

CONFETTI

Between my next breath
and my last
is a grand box
of confetti

Silent garden around me
designs on a stone fence
I only want to see
memories through a soft lens

Soft whiff of wisteria
honey on my gums
silence in a hot air balloon
smell of cinnamon buns

Deep down throaty laugh
seltzer bubbles on my tongue
feeling of a silk scarf
warm wet Tahiti toes

TO CUT

Middle of February
fifty nine at noon
my skinny hand hurt
bending fingers to cut

sharp cold stems
between bougainvillea thorns
tiny daggers
blood on parchment

tired wrist
knuckled stubborn thumb
as long as scissors work
I will cut what I love

CLOUDS

Clouds are
in praise of Florida mountains
that hug horizons
and lure us toward them.

They are there, not consistently
but dependably,
they disperse creeping shadows
and quick showers.

Clouds expand our vistas
hide planes,birds, smoke
and give us horizon mountains,
sometimes chinchilla collars

"If you don't like

something, change it.

If you can't change it,

change your attitude.

Don't complain."

Maya Angelou

D

Don't fuss with love - it's fundamental.

Don't step on my shadow or my reflection.

Don't squander the small joys of anything.

Do not waste new tears on old grief.

Don't live in a world of one color.

Don't let the first snow catch you unprepared.

Do what needs to be done without regret.

Destiny and choice are friends.

Don't meddle with a man doing a good job.

DEATH AT HIGH NOON

Ghosts float there
like wrinkled wash
words hung in the air
haunted echoes
lonely came and sat
next to empty
same old story
new players repeat music
did love leave quietly gently
no, it rushed angrily
with foam, frustration
reflective days empty nights -
lost communication
you breathed, ate, laid there
a letter arrived from a lawyer
it ended with a Forever stamp.

E

Eyes can look in many directions, so can minds.

Be extraordinary once in a while.

What the eye sees is not necessarily so.

Excel in something.

Be an excellent friend.

Excess anything could cause a problem.

The mind's eye is not always right.

Every day is a clean slate.

Extend yourself. It is a wise investment.

F

Foolishness is reparable.

Frustration solves nothing. Act.

Fun is for everyone. Try some.

A friend is three dimensional love.

Fun is a thrill you can feel.

Freedom is not free.
We pay for it one way or another.

Don't flaunt anything.

If you fish with a net know the depth of the water.

Forbidden fruit is really rotten in the core.

Make sure the face one presents to
others is not a mask.

FORSYTHIA

Bursts upon Spring

with

Spring spears

decorating

among tulips and daffodils,

bushes

spring sprays gardens

dazzling

swaying yellow

G

Government – we expect our country to run efficiently on national, state, county and city levels.

THAT IT RUNS AT ALL IS A MIRACLE.

Gauntlet - don't pick one up unless you are prepared to do so.

Good health is happiness.

God is there whether you know it or not.

Goodness is not next to Godliness.

Goodbye is not the end of the world.
Sometimes it opens a door.

Get going! What does standing around accomplish.

Don't fool around with God. You'll lose.

H

He wanted more bells and sirens on the boat
so the money multiplied.

Happiness is born to be shared, enjoyed, but
never consumed.

Happiness is a risk.

Happiness is a product of giving not receiving.

Happiness is when you vaguely hear the garbage truck
at 5:30 a.m. and immediately go back to sleep.

Happiness is making the toilet when you really
have to go!

Harvest moon walking across the pond of memory.

Hailstones glancing off the roof like troubles leaning
on their canes.

Happiness is having a short memory.

Happiness needs to be shared.

Hate is expensive. Why pay for any.

Happiness is the ability to cope with conflict.

HAPPINESS CAN HAPPEN IN LITTLE PLACES

HANDS

I awoke partly and moved my hand which touched her side. In a moment she placed her hand like a glove into mine.

An intimate moment lingered and slowly my hand warmed, became hot, the back of my hand under pressure.

At that moment my wife's hand moved away. My hand cooled. I lay there, cuddled that glove feeling and drifted into a sleep of turquoise blue on a Bermuda reef which surrounded a brick floored restaurant with a wobbly table.

Our soup moved as we ate it.

I wondered where my wife's mind was now.

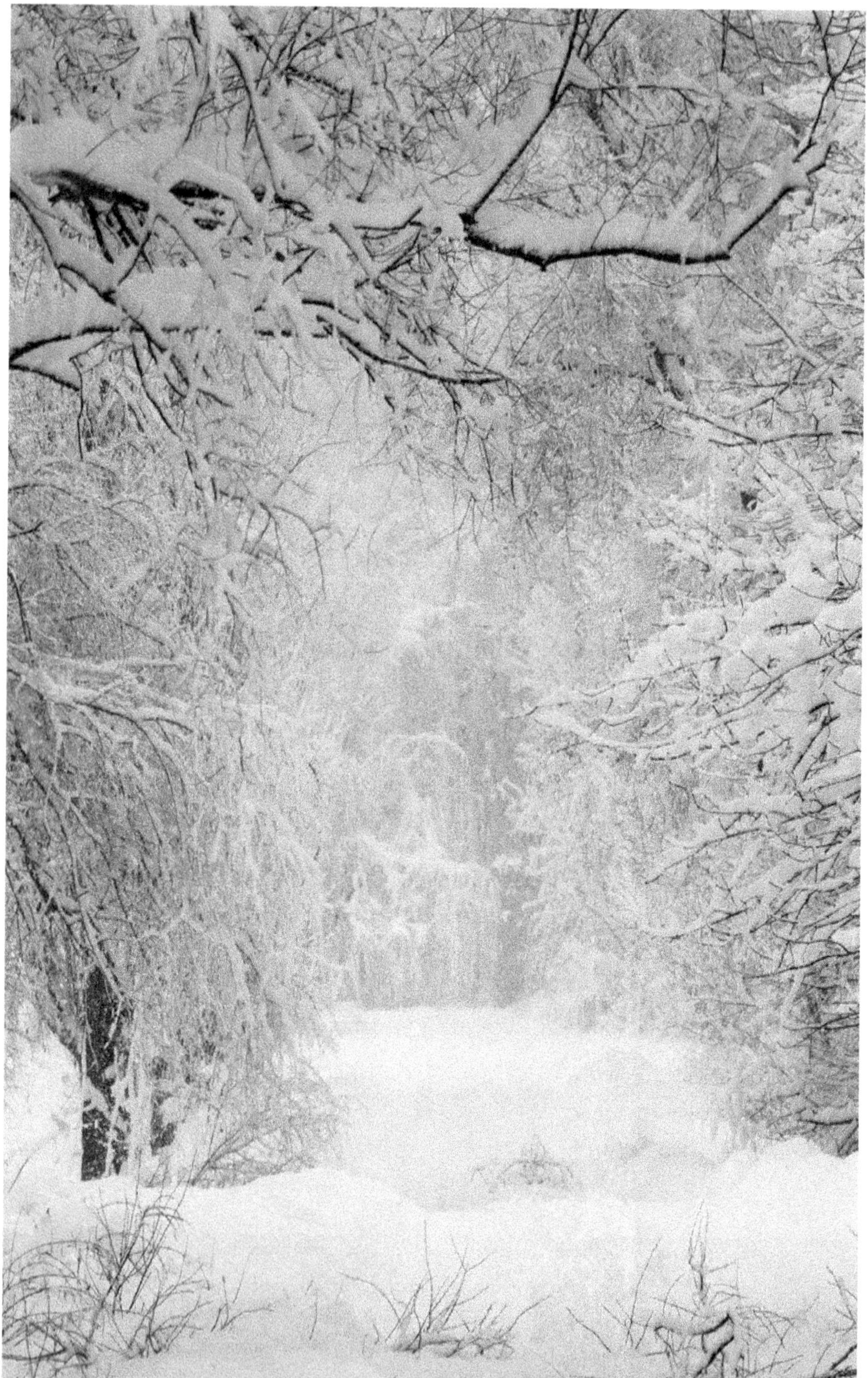

WHAT IS A HAIKU?

"Sharing is one of the things we want most out of life, to give something of ourselves to others so that they might accept us and our experiences and perceptions as important. Haiku gives an impression of who we are, some piece of the story of our lives."*

*The haiku handbook- Higginson and Harter, page 47

COMMENTS FROM THE AUTHOR

Haikus are not goodness, truth or beauty. They are brief encounters interpreted by the writer's mind.

Haiku, the very short, three line poem, has been created in Japan since the middle 1600s. Haiku share small intimate feelings, objects, or events and lets people see things from a different point of view. Haiku reflects nature and our five senses.

Seeing - a little more than meets the eye.

Hearing - the parts of a symphony.

Smelling - ingredients of a recipe.

Feelings - a concerto of memories.

Touching - those textures in life.

Silent swift easy shot.
Agony of soft grey fluff
drops like a thrown stone.

Evening silhouette.
That sparrow makes a lazy shape
around a new moon.

Not small, about half big -
poor child ties string to a hook,
food for the pot, maybe.

A warm dead rabbit.
Scavengers scurry to it,
a grateful handout.

Those trees hung with snow
shook themselves on a cold breeze.
They awakened dawn.

Chirping cricket sits
in that scarecrow stovepipe hat
waiting for some answer.

We want to know life
it does not go into words
but it surrounds us.

Our smoking memory
what does that help to resolve
now that things are done.

Firmament furnace
stoked by sizzling clouds
linger tenderly.

Young proud aspen army
never humbled by any mountains
that can never bend.

A cloudless sunset
is like a fingerless dawn,
you have only one color.

The spade-split anthill
exposed scurrying black cities
under a muddy boot.

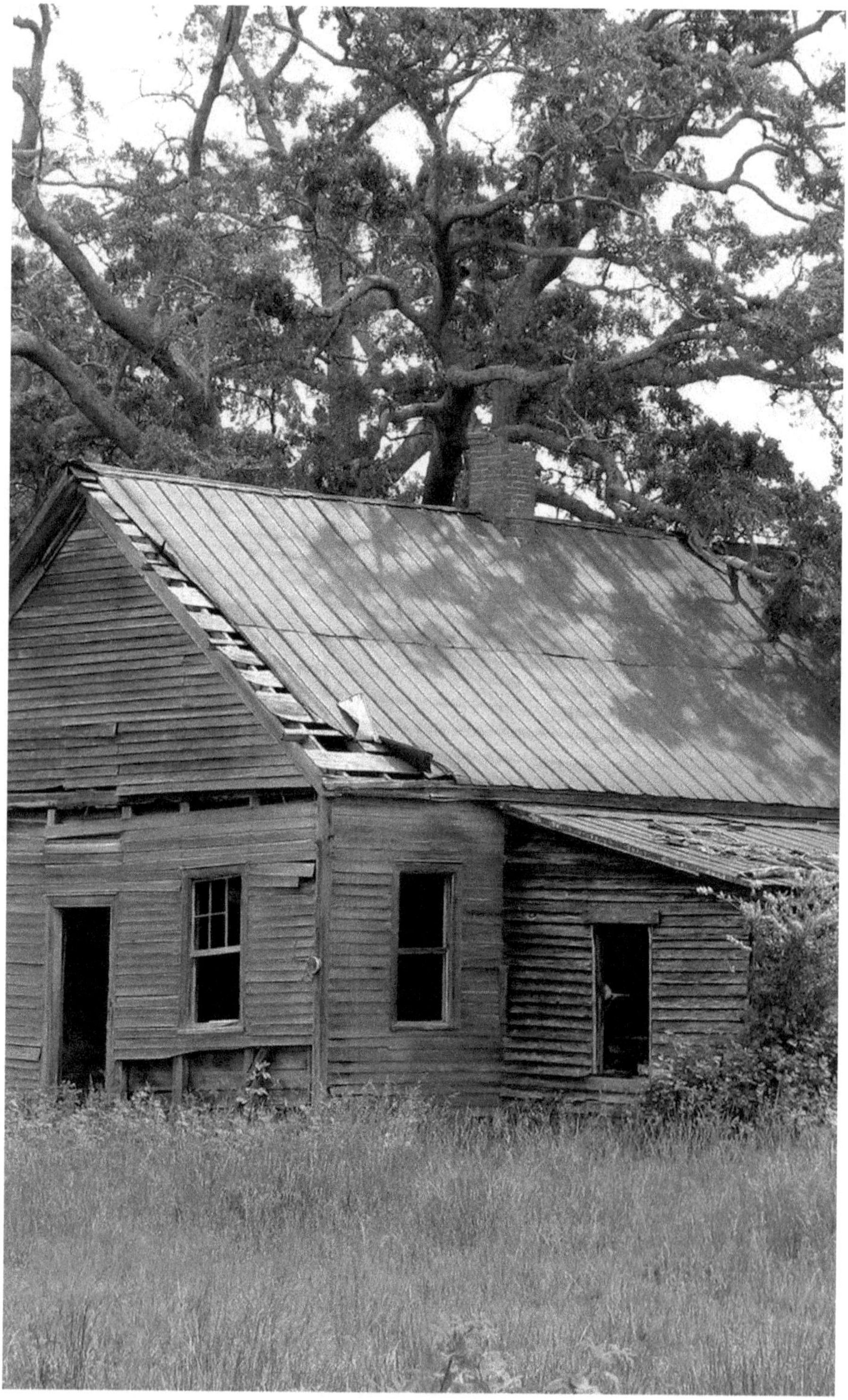

On the streams bottom
the faint shadow of an eel
resting on gray sand.

Unique red water bridge
silently guards her fortress –
oblique authority.

Dawn walks the beach
early footprints disappear,
ripples lap each shape.

Calliope fades,
the soft fall wind still echoes
a melody there.

The breeze looks for me.
Bunches of hungry weeds hide
from my strong fingers.

Silent color echoes
fall upon grass like freckles
bamboo teeth fetch them.

Heavy winter clouds
quieted away softly
to hide in the grey hills.

At high noon summer
a gull sails quietly passed
not moving its wings.

Worn sneakers feel good
warm against old flat field stones
a smooth autumn color.

In an empty room
one feather lifts carefully
and floats over that duct.

After a soft spring rain
that precious damp green earth smell
lingers in a shadow.

The sharp cold so fierce
it bit the shadows on snow,
a spring reminder.

JAPANESE HAIKU MASTERS

Haiku began in the great age of renga, poems linked by several group poets in the seventeenth century.

Matsuo Basko (1644-1699 made his living traveling around teaching classes the art and craft of writing renga. He wrote haiku as an introduction for a renga. He became famous for his haiku. Unusual.

Yosa Buson (1716-1784 was a painter. His haiku verses have a sensual and objective quality we can accept from a painter. In all his work he brought form and a love of shape, color and movement.

Kobayashi Issa (1762-1826 was a country bumpkin compared to the ascetic, worldly, sophisticated Buson. Issa grew up in the country and was banished to city poverty by a cruel stepmother. He came to prefer the company of small insignificant creatures.

Masaoka Shiki (1807-1902). Renga died out as a serious art form. Shiki concentrated on haiku. He was seriously ill with spinal tuberculoses and died at age thirty-five. He wrote of quiet, loneliness and tranquility.

Glittery hailstones
gleaning off the tin shed roof
on a scarecrows hat.

Strong slim slingshot tree
conceals tiny butterfly eggs
with pale green web ferns.

This tired cold year gone
new direction for my shoes
hat on my head.

Mayonnaise pickles
hot noon shoulders on a bench –
– that trickle of sweat.

HAIKU

A POINT OF VIEW

EVERY HAIKU I WRITE
IS TRUTH AND FICTION.

ONCE YOU PUT WORDS
ON PAPER YOU CHOOSE
WHAT TO SAY
WHAT NOT TO SAY
AND HOW TO SAY IT.

TRUTH AND FICTION

When winds thump and bump
thunder rain hail snow about
caution soon leaves.

Wash on a tight line -
carriage of beanie babies
sat on the old porch.

In autumn's evening
neglected vegetables mope
among sleeping weeds.

Weathered forlorn
shanty town shanty sat there,
memories gone too.

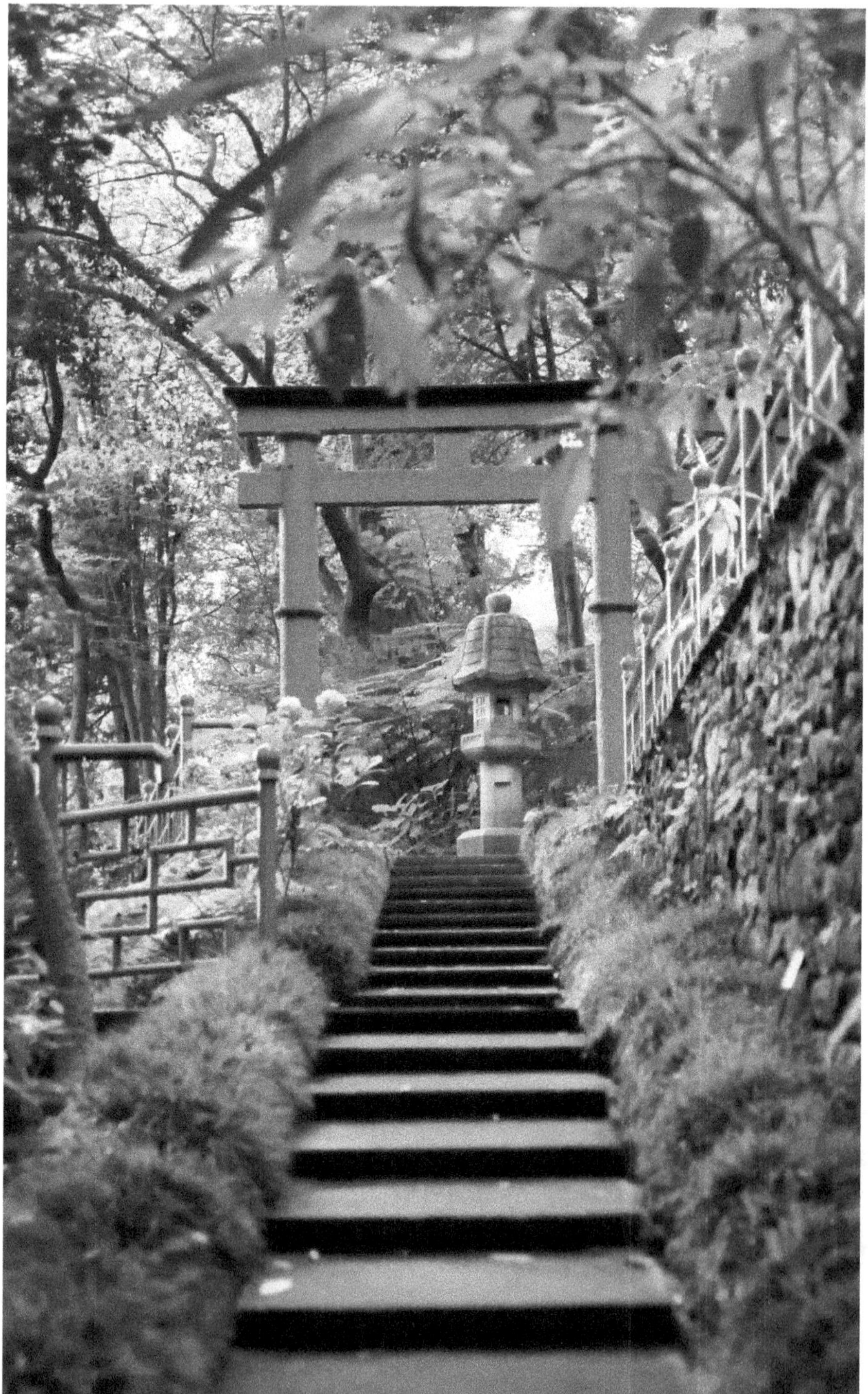

Disheveled white hair
window sill teeth on the floor
that never wore smiles.

In that quiet dark
scrawny cart dragging along
vegetables in the straw.

Quiet smooth blue lake
reflects soft chinchilla puffs.
Oblique pearl necklace.

No other distractions
those fireworks sounding far away
why do I expect more?

Brilliant moonlight
dark clouds above sling-shot pine
surprise drops finished.

Casual cruising
mosquitoes buzz in moist air
perfumed ear beckons.

Late languid autumn
commingles with lingering heat
chaffed by the wind.

Coal mine work whistle
three yellow pretentious eggs
sit staring upward.

HAIKU

SOMETIMES

THINK

VEGETABLE SOUP

RATHER THAN

MEAT STEW

HE

HELD FAITH

IN

HIS HEART

LIKE STARS

I

If you are really enthusiastic about your life
you are happy!

If you really want to do it, no matter what,
nobody can stop you.

If you are not curious about life, you miss it.

If the world slips a little - slide along.

If you have a good life - you earned it.

If you have a fantastic dream, don't wake up
right away.

If you love what you do - you are successful.

If you squander your dreams, you wind up poor.

If you are wiser than others do not tell them
or show it.

If you want to give happiness, smile.

If your house is struck by lightening –
stay where you are, it never strikes twice.

It's courage that counts.

INNOCENTS

It was a big box -
heavy, corrugated, re-enforced.
Refrigerators were delivered in them,
left on the sidewalk for trash.

I was not seven but more than six.
Forever friends, Henry, Billy, Lindy and me.
We four - Mutt and Jeff twice,
dragged the box to the long alley next to my house.

We played with armies of little soldiers
cowboys, indians, pirates, people and animals
in that paved alley - so free at six.
Great escapades with toy figures. Our minds soared.

Exploits before astronauts,
moon walks, gravity or weightlessness.
We didn't know what space was.
Adventures, yes, other worlds, no.

We had a corner lot for rough house and mumbledee peg.
Back watched the zoo we found in clouds.
Our paved street used for roller skates,
kick -the-can, red rover, and hide and seek.

But we returned to our special box over and over.
A submarine, prairie schooner, airplane,
fort or medieval castle provided exotic adventure.
We were our own heroes.

Our group married but we four socialized alone.
Ball games, bars, poker, fishing, camping, hunting.
We liked our own company. We talked or we were quiet.
We knew us thoroughly.

It worked out poorly.
A car accident killed Billy at twenty nine.
Henry died at forty two. Cause unknown.
Lindy's wife left him for a woman at fifty.

I have lived the good, bad, absurd war,
death, divorce, recession, illness and age.
I am often surprised at the long littleness of life.
Oh, that big box that made us happy and fearless.

J

Just occasionally do what you want to do, when you want to do it, how you want to do it.

Joy is a prism of life's colors.

Real joy is making it yourself.

Joy is contagious. Start an epidemic.

Joy moves in mysterious ways.

Joy does not come in a bottle, box or book. It's inside.

Justice is for everyone, but it is so slow.

Jealousy is jaded.

HIS NAME IS JOHNNY

His name was Juan Hernandes but everyone called him Johnny, except his family. He was about six when we met. I was about twenty-six, sixty years ago.

My dad had a small linen service business. No domestic laundry. Doctors, dentists, hotels, restaurants, gas stations, hand towels on a ring in the toilets. It was located in a lower middle class white neighborhood, all building went right up to the sidewalk which were four to five feet wide.

We lived a mile and a half due north of there so I could walk home after school from my job of killing cockroaches in the dirty laundry that our trucks collected from clients. I did this every afternoon after school and usually two hours on Saturday mornings for $.02 per roach! I earned movie, spending and gift money.

I was a traveling art teacher in grades one to six in New Brunswick, New Jersey where I first taught Johnny. He lived around the corner from my Dad's laundry business.

Sometimes after school my mother phoned me to bring home a loaf of bread or two bananas from our local store. I gave Johnny a lollypop, a stick of gum or a nickel if he would go to the store for me.

Johnny never watched me kill roaches. In an odd way we became friends. He volunteered to help wash the business trucks or clean many business windows. For many years I gave Johnny money to go to the Saturday cheap movie matinee.

As Johnny grew up he always found me one or two times during my teaching week. We touched base. He was always polite, reliable and considerate.

He had no art skills! When he was sixteen he told me he was quitting school, getting a factory job. He needed to help his two younger siblings with clothes, field trips or spending money. Girls flocked around him so he needed more money.

"You will keep in touch."

"Of course."

and he always did.

When he was twenty he arrived at my door.

"Hello. I hear you have an apartment for rent."

"How did you know that?" I replied.

"Around here everybody knows everything." said Johnny.

That was true. He looked well, a bit taller and very well dressed.

"It won't be available until the first," I replied.

I told him the rent. He gave me one months security and the first months' rent - September.

Johnny was a good tenant. Clean, quiet, rent on time. About ten months' later he came to my door in a suit and tie. "You look well." I said.

"I am seeing a lady."

"And"

"I would like her to live with me."

"Good. When would you like to bring her over for dinner?"

She came and conquered. Bright, interesting, alert.

She had been a beautician for two years working in a shop with a good reputation. Her sister was going to graduate from high school in one year. She would also go to beautician school. They had the name picked out for their beauty shop. She and Johnny were perfect together.

During the next five or six weeks they furnished the three room upper front apartment. The furniture wasn't cheap or expensive. It was very well done.

Johnny visited his mother often. On a Saturday morning I saw his almost new shiny car next to her home.

"Hello Johnny," I said. "How are things going?"

"Good, Mr. Kahrmann."

Long pause – I had the answer.

"No wedding for now"

"Why?"

"We don't think we're ready."

He stiffened. I pursued my direction.

"Ready for what? A future, a commitment, a plan."

"That's none of your business."

"Normally you would be right. However, there are a few existing circumstances."

"Such as?"

"You are not renting an apartment just anywhere, you are renting an apartment in a building I own. It is also my home and has been since long before you were born."

Johnny looked at me, nodded, and took a short step back. He got the message.

"I like your lady. You are lucky to have found her but you may meet someone else down the road and then another etc. There will never be revolving women in your apartment. Is that clear?"

"Yes, it's clear." Johnny said.

And there never was. Less than a year later she was gone. No replacements. Johnny took his business elsewhere.

All went quietly. Sometimes he invited my wife and me to his apartment for dinner. We invited him to dinner occasionally.

One night a neighbor that I had know for years knocked on my door.

"Hello Tom," I said. "Come in."

Tom came in.

"Sit down," I said.

"No, this won't take long," said Tom.

"Juan lives upstairs front. He has his private front entrance?' "Yes," I nodded.

"You can see cars or people from his front living room window?"

"Yes."

"Juan is selling drugs. He sees a buyer, buses him inside and sells hard stuff - cocaine and heroine."

I was stunned!

"How do you know this?"

"Neighbors have figured it out."

"How long has this been going on?"

"A while."

Silence!

"There is more."

"What?"

"The neighbors think you knew about this and are getting a cut." A long silence.

"Why didn't they tell the police?'

"We 've known your family and you a long time, nobody wants to tell."

"I'll do something! I don't know how or when."

This was Thursday evening. My wife and I talked and decided to knock on his door Sunday at 2 p.m. If no answer we would leave him a note to phone us.

Sunday my brother phone me and told me to look at an article on the bottom of page five. The article said,

DRUG DEALER KILLED

I had to make a sympathy call on neighbors that I could see from my kitchen window.

JOAN

Big things do not bind
mend fix repair
familiar casual conversations
what is said what is meant

Decision to watch
a T.V. program
either or
nobody wins

Cutting her toenails
touching hands in the night
washing her comb and brush
going to a restaurant I like

Attitudes that stay
between latitudes
soft phone call
that warms

I

Encourages me to buy a shirt I like
but don't need
lobster juice on our chins
her lingering smile in a casino

Ordinary moments cement
looking at travel folders
pills, glass of water
message to remind me

Marriage is not what we thought
but what it is
we mend the sad, impossible
we caress the magic

2

LIFE

IS OVER THERE

SEEK IT

FIND

ITS JOYS

JIME HILTON

The city is a contrast in beauty and dirt. Beautiful beaches and open sewers where drunks sometimes fall in and drown. If the breeze is in a particular direction a foul odor from the open market of decomposed fish, meat, fruit and vegetables prevail. This is Cartagena, Columbia, due south of Miami on the Caribbean with four seasons of three months each. Two seasons with comfortable weather and two that are not. There are rich and poor people. Some are educated, some are not. Some have a future, most do not.

The city is flat, surrounded by thick high protective walls with Spanish Colonial architecture, cobble stone streets reflecting its beginning in the early fifteenth century when Spain and England ruled the seas. A menacing fort sits on top of a hill guarding the city. Cartagena is not a typical Spanish outpost.

My friend Jime Velez was not a typical anything. He was wealthy from tobacco, cattle and bananas. Jime had three houses. One in Cartagena, one in Bogota. one in Cali. Three of his five children were in an American Oil Company K-8 school in Cartagena. I was the principal of this school. Jime and I met three years earlier when my wife and I arrived in Cartagena. We bonded rapidly.

One Tuesday Jime phoned my office and invited me to join him early Friday morning for a three day journey into the jungle so that he could purchase land to grow more bananas.

We stopped for lunch and a clearing was hacked away by a

machete quickly and efficiently. I dismounted in pain but smiling while Jime watched the scene. I offered to help with lunch, Jime shook his head. Food was a repeat of breakfast. All ate in silence on the jungle floor in a semi-circle. Jime sat crossed-legged beside me on my left with a gun near his knee. Juan was on my right, a machete at hand I saw bugs, snakes. lizards. spiders, rats and other jungle creatures as we chewed our food. Someone made a smart remark. Everyone laughed except Jime.

Jime said in Spanish, "He is a good man with a warm heart and my friend." I understood he was speaking of me.

"A compadre?" one asked.

"Yes," Jime replied.

We rode on another hour or so until I saw to my horror mules in front of us. Jime got off his horse and helped me dismount. I was a cripple.

Jime questioned, "You've ridden a mule?"

"Yes, to the bottom of the Grand Canyon and back up. It's hell on four legs."

"Are you up to it?"

"I have to be. I may hate you forever."

Jime laughed. Above me was a unique view of various species of five foot tall fems with bromeliads sprinkled among them, orchids on gnarled branches with monkeys chattering. The canopy created shades of green, blues, and yellows dappled with sunlight. There was a smell of healthy decay. I was dazzled.

A dirty pickup truck was waiting and the four of us climbed in. There were boxes of supplies, a spare tire, tools and rope for measuring as we rumbled along for about two hours on a dirt road. We slowed and stopped at the rear of two large jeeps to transfer our gear, have a pee and swig of rum. On we drove at a fast clip on land that had begun to be hilly. We slowed down at the foothills to the Andes Mountains and stopped. There were two men and five horses awaiting us. Two horses were loaded with gear from the truck. The three remaining horses were loaded and we mounted.

Jime helped me up on this beast with a smile. He knew I had never been on a horse.

"Just hold the reins," Jime said. "The horse will do everything."

I asked, "What about running, jumping and forging streams?"

"The horse will take care of that."

"My ass," I said.

Jime answered. "You take care of that yourself!"

The horses were smelly, dirty. and middle-aged. I bobbed up and down in the saddle to the amusement of all. looking ridiculous, nervous and a bit frightened. That was rapidly replace by thigh, ankles, back. bottom, neck and shoulder aches, plus tall bushes and low small branches that scratched me. Approaching noon. my eyes swept the variety of flowers, ferns, vines, bushes and trees. Spectacular, but wild and dangerous.

We striped, jumped into the stream, gasping because of the shock of the frigid water. My legs and feet were numb. Rapidly we soaped down. rinsed ourselves and we were dried by the sun and breeze. Dressed in clean, damp clothes we returned to the plateau where rum warmed us.

Thirty minutes later Jime and two men left camp with weapons, rope. rum and food to stake out the plots for growing bananas. A third man, an Indian who lived in a thatched hut on the opposite end of the plateau, followed them at a respectful distance. I sat on a log and wrote in my journal, then I went into the hut to find my paperback novel and saw the Indian's wife who was straightening up. She was thin. with purple black hair that was filthy. She had big eyes and few teeth that were dirty. Her age was vague, twenty-ish. I smiled. She nodded and studied me. It probably was my light, bleached by the sun wavy hair. and tortoise shell eyeglasses. I went into the kitchen and saw a hanging piece of meat dripping blood with flies and mosquitoes on it. That was the pork we had for supper last evening.

After wandering around the plateau I read my book sitting on a stump. Later I sauntered toward the tiny hut with poles holding up a thatched roof with the two side walls. Here was a small fire plus strange, muffled little sounds. At that moment a naked three year old boy appeared from the jungle. We sized each other up. He stood his ground, but would not let me touch him. The little sound continued. Glancing up to the smoky level above me I saw a hanging basket. The sound was a baby's cough caused by the smoke. While I was attempting to show the mother that the baby should be on a lower level without polluted air Jime appeared. He looked. We walked away.

"It's gorgeous."

"What is?" Jime asked

"That," I said, sweeping my eyes around the jungle.

Jime looked at me thoughtfully. "You noticed?" he said with a small smile.

We mounted the mules which walked in a straight line perfumed constantly by plopping dung and a variety of noises accompanied by gasses which gave us a very loud, unique "Grand Canyon Suite." Finally, I could not stand the saddle one more moment. I painfully slid off this offensive creature.

Jime watched, "Take hold of his tail"

I did what I was told and found it was a big help to be pulled up by this beast up the side of the hill. What I did not know was the mule could have kicked me in the knee. Jime's eyes were usually on me.

At early dusk, we arrived at a jungle plateau which had been cut clean and cleared with one building. All dismounted. I could barely move but I had an immediate problem.

"Jime, I need a toilet," I said.

He went into a building, returning with a roll of toilet paper and a red shovel. He tossed me the paper and handed me the shovel.

"Out there," he said.

This was my first experience at the Jime Hilton. When

I returned I saw the building made of mud bricks, dirt floors, thatched roof. two rooms - one for cooking and one for eating, sleeping and drinking with empty door frames and windows.

From the kitchen area I heard the drip drip of water and wonderful smells of food cooking. Suddenly paper cups with rum, crackers in a plain box and pieces of yellow cheese appeared. We sat on cut off pieces of tree trunks around a small table upon which were plastic plates and utensils. Paper towels were napkins. We sat down to a marvelous supper of port, corn on the cob, fried plantains, rice with delicate spices and a very cool soda. I held up the frosted can.

Jime said, "We have invented a refrigerator."

"My compliments to the chef," I answered.

"It's not the Hilton." He smiled.

"It is to me."

Jime gave me a calculated, thoughtful look, but said nothing. Before bedtime we sat in companionable silence.

"Why is your English so perfect?" I finally asked him. "Where did you learn it?"

"Between the sheets," he replied.

I laughed. Then I realized he was serious.

"You're not joking." I said.

"It's true. There are many lovely wives of American naval officers in Cartagena. While the husbands played with their vessels I played with their wives."

I smiled, lit a cigarette, poured each of us a small rum and sat back down.

I said, "Why don't you go to the States?"

"I have been to the states. My sister lives there. I can't go back."

"Why not?"

"Because of a woman's husband."

"A lovely mysterious lady."

"A very special lady," Jime said in a tender, thoughtful, caressing voice.

"That serious?"

"Yes, that serious."

"You met love?"

"Her husband caught us, he knew I was rich, powerful and politically aligned. If he made a fuss his career, family and future would be destroyed. There were two beautiful children who would also be victims. I had my own wife, five children and a career."

"A tragedy," I said.

"More of a disaster."

"So it ended?"

"Not quite."

"What happened?"

Jime got up and lit three candles with his lighter, poured himself a rum, gave one to Juan and sat down sipping his drink.

"The husband phoned me and asked to meet me in the patio bar at the Hotel Cari be for a drink at 4:30 p.m. He and his wife were seated when I arrived. 'Good afternoon!' The naval officer said."

I nodded.

Jime said, "The Commander said two things - 'You will swear to never see or write to or speak to each other again.' He then put a small bible on the table and we swore."

Jime whispered, "The husband said, 'Jime, if you ever come to the States, you will be killed.' They got up from the table and left the hotel."

There was a long silence. Jime didn't move and his face was in deep shadow. I poured him another rum. The candles sputtered. Juan lit a lamp and hammocks were hung. I realized he'd heard this conversation.

I decided to sleep on the floor, so a man brought in a very large bag of com cobs, which he dumped in a corner, placing three layers of burlap bags on top of them. The tiny bed was refined torture along with strange smells, noises, sounds, and the symphony from the mules.

Eventually dawn came accompanied by roosters, pigs, goats, parrots, and monkey sounds. Breakfast was canned juice. powered milk, cereal and honey, plus fruit and coffee. Jime finished his coffee and stretched. He was six feet tall, muscular, broad shoulders, slim but wiry with dark hair, olive skin and piercing brown eyes under heavy dark smooth eyebrows. He moved like a panther. I remember the naval officer's threat and decided I wouldn't want to tangle with Jime.

"Bath time," he said.

We got our soap, change of clothes and walked single file through a vague path in the jungle for about four long blocks arriving at a wide clear stream with flat rocks on each side. We bathed and put on fresh clothes.

"I tried to explain about the smoke to the Indian."

"I know."

"What will happen to the baby?"

"He will die in a day or two."

"But..."

"There are no buts," Jime said. "It's the toss of the dice. He could be you and you could be him."

He put his arm around my shoulder and we walked slowly back to the Hilton. I was hot. We went to the frigid stream and got two cokes, then sat in the shade. I looked at Jime and he knew what I was going to say.

"She's Commander Valdez's wife, Lydia," I said. He nodded.

"How did you know?"

"I guessed. You always start at the top."

"Unfortunately."

"When did this happen?"

"One month before you arrived. They left Cartagena shortly after that."

"And you never communicated?"

"Never."

"Are you going to?"

"I don't know."

"You do know? When you come to the States contact me. I'll do what I can to help."

"One more thing."

"Yes?"

"Wear an American business suit. A hat, umbrella, and raincoat would be useful."

That night as I lay on the corn cobs my mind went over yesterday's trip to this plateau. At dawn we would repeat the journey home and I dreaded the prospect. As it turned out it was a disaster.

While I was riding on a horse, a poisonous snake fell from a branch dangerously lose to my face. Then later while getting off the back of the pickup truck, I tripped on a root and in bracing myself for the fall, l hit hard on my arm on another part of the same root. Jime was next to me in seconds.

"It's broken," he said.

"I can tell."

"Bad?"

"Bad enough."

"Is the car gassed?" Jime asked Juan.

The limousine loaded, Jime asked me which direction to go. I told him to Cartagena. As we traveled this straight road at great speed, Jime said nothing. From time to time a road bump jarred the car which felt like we went over a boulder. I made no sound. Jime gave me swigs of rum during the journey. Somewhere along the way I realized I was drunk. I opened my eyes saw that the hospital was nearby and looked at Jime.

"Thank you for this weekend." I said.

"Sorry you broke your arm."

"You play the cards you've got.

We arrived at the Emergency door with Jime on one side of me and Juan on the other. They maneuvered me through the swinging door. Immediately I focused on a familiar face. She looked at me with recognition, disdain, annoyance, and contempt.

A small figure with a bandaged hand said, "Hello Mr. Kahrmann."

"Hello Maria," I answered with a weak smile.

A wheel chair arrived, I sat down carefully with help while a pillow was placed gently under my arm. At that exact moment I recognized Señora Vega, Maria's mother, the suspicious, gossipy battle axe who was president of my school's Parent-Teacher Association. She was glaring at me. Jime knew her. When I looked at him his lips were a smirk. As the nurse wheeled me past Señora Vega I threw up on her shoes and pocketbook. I could hear the commotion while Jime laughed.

I thought about school at 7:00 a.m. tomorrow. It was Sunday morning now. Cartagena is a small town. Jime and I were very well known. Everyone would know this story by tomorrow morning and it would be a pip!! Very far from the truth and juicy with scandal. My entire body ached. My arm hurt. my head hurt, my bottom hurt, and I threw up again on the x-ray technician.

K

Kindness is – my pills are next to my juice at breakfast

when people really listen to me when I speak

listening to someone tell the story again

helping when you are needed

holding a door for anyone

giving directions

sincerely inquiring about someone's health

knowing when to listen

phoning someone who is ill

driving someone who can't

L

Life is a series of moments. Don't waste them.

Live the width of your life - it is better than the length.

Love is my wife who covers me up on a cool night.

Liars need a good memory.

Life is slippery. Take my hand.

Love is my wife offering me choices for breakfast.

Lie once – you'll lie twice.

Life is what we ourselves make it.

Life "ain't necessarily so."

LUNCH

One day in August, 1960 in the very hot, humid, filthy port city of Guayaquil, Ecuador, South America I went to a hotel for a quick lunch before flying back to Quito, the capitol.

A small shabby gloomy dining room with chipped tile floor welcomed me with flies and a few mosquitoes. I knew hungry cockroaches were loitering.

After ordering food, I asked the waiter in sign language for the toilet. He pointed to a door at the end of the room in the middle of the wall. I entered and saw the toilet was like those I had often seen in European bars, bistro or public toilets. Two raised pedestals just the right height and position for your feet. Placing your feet on them you squat and do your business in a hole between the two pedestals. A cord hanging from the ceiling was pulled to flush it. Water came rushing over the floor to clean and flush.

This particular flush brought much more water than needed for this four foot square toilet area. Suddenly water ran over my shoes.

I exited rapidly as water ran out of my shoes, my trousers bottoms wet. I had the attention of the dining room as a cockroach crawled out of my trouser cuff and up my pants leg.

LIFE IS SLIPPERY TAKE SOMEONE'S HAND

LIFE
GIVES US GOOD
BAD
SOMETIMES
WONDERFUL

M

Make a big deal out of wonderful little things.

My house partly clean, partly dirty - is what it is.

Moonlight seeps through the thicket of birch, searching.

Mothers surround us with illuminated love.

Moonlight softens the eye with delicate perspective.

Mothers are cushions we land upon when we fall.

Man cannot help another without helping himself.

The measure of a man takes time.

Do not meddle - you don't have the right.

If you are going to meditate anything get all the facts.

MOMENT

Walking along a road in Lee
after
a downpour
a quarter in a puddle
abundance
in one second.

The world not altered
air was not
crisper
a rustle of the leaves lost no music
life
gave no considering eye.

Yellow buttercups and cowslips
amid
soft thunder rumbles
life unconsciously squandered
no new wet coin in a puddle gutter
no treasure from rain today.

That silver shiny quarter
slept
one ear open
in an old
half closed dark painted drawer
of an old chest.

Memories

remain

in a heart

like a family

of ghosts

MARCH TAVERN
A Summer Memoir

I was an only child, age ten. My family's house in the city had six small rooms on an average street, very different from the March Tavern house, which was nestled on an aged, occasionally traveled road, on an island next to Newburyport, Massachusetts, at the mouth of the Merimack River. A wide creek ran between the island and the mainland. You could wade in it, swim in it, or drive over it.

We got out of the car on June 30ıh and four parents plus two children greeted each other. But I saw only the house. It looked like a huge white monolith. March Tavern sat low on the ground next to an ancient track now made into a narrow country lane which had been a horse path and earlier a trail. The house was two-storied, had a center hall with four large rooms on each level and eight fireplaces. I walked through the front door, down the long hall, across the rear veranda, down the lawn and stood on a dike with the marshes, the sky, and the river in front of me. I fell in love with that house.

Having delivered me, four days later my parents departed. I was ensconced there for six weeks with my Aunt Agnes, a rather prissy, dull lady, my cousin Ruth, quiet, pleasant, domestic with a lovely personality and Uncle Bill. He was warm, kind, and generous of his time and skills. He had always wanted a son. He taught me to sail, fish, shoot a rifle and play poker. I learned that ordinary stamps could be a history lesson. We walked along the dikes, at the end of the back yard while Uncle Bill taught me about tides and marshes.

Another inhabitant of March Tavern was two year old Laddie, a large white collie with a brown spot as big as a fifty cent piece on his chest, under his chin. Laddie adored Uncle Bill. When my uncle went to work, Laddie never let me out of his sight. I was his playmate. He was my friend.

March Tavern was built in 1690, as the only stage coach stop between Boston and Bangor, Maine. Immediate local history was repetitive. Travel when necessary, build a house, plant crops, hunt or fish. Join a new settlement if possible or start one if this is where you want to settle. Local jobs were reasons for settlements. Newburyport had an early fishing boat industry, plus lumber, seafood, trapping and fur trading. Eventually whaling bought in large amounts of people, money, and industry. A meager village slowly became significant Newburyport town.

Any stagecoach journey to Bangor, Maine left the March Tavern at dawn after a night's sleep and food, rode four blocks and was loaded upon a log raft and pulled across the Merrimack River by ropes. Bangor was a predictable day and one half journey.

Foot, horse, wagon or stagecoach travel was slow and difficult, especially in cold months. Erratic weather sometimes three or four kinds in one ten or twelve hour day was normal. A few pit stops for changing, feeding, watering or replacing a horseshoe. A bowl of soup, coffee and an outhouse were always welcome for those wayfarers who sat on boxes in a wood structure next to a fire for twenty minutes or so.

The eight March Tavern fireplaces were huge. Two were used for cooking. the others for heat. Three of them had a narrow mantle for grog mugs. The floors were varied wide boards painted light grey with splatters of black and white dots. Only the kitchen was light pumpkin with yellow and white splatters. The windows were six over six. High up a widows walk to watch for returning ships. In a beam a thick chain tethered slaves in a small room over one end of the kitchen with a narrow ladder between the beams for entry, air, and heat.

The dikes were always a challenge. How far I could travel jumping across them at dead low tide, the creatures who lived on or in them and the heady, salty, pungent and unique assortment of smells. Other natural smells were special: dirt, hay, sea spray, cut grass, but a salt dike odor mixed with a sea breeze, clouds, sun and seagulls is suspended in my memory.

One day I discovered pure clay in a dike. This new material was a challenge. Ruth and I and other kids on our street soon learned you could make animals, people, flowers, small bowls and paperweights. However, jewelry fascinated all of us. We learned clay techniques from each other experimenting in using a rolling pin, knife, stringing beads of clay together to make necklaces with a needle and fishing line. We used various small objects and incised designs into the clay, breast plates (Aztec) were a favorite item. Dry clay could be tempera painted and shellacked.

Wearing our jewelry with costumes and props, we made up stories of kings, queens, knights, explorers, sea captains, evil warriors, under sea worlds and palaces.

Up the road about a mile was the creek swimming hole. It was equally divided by a sturdy bridge. The boys swam there bare assed. One day we were frolicking at the end of the creek, our clothes at the other. My cousin Ruth crept up and stole our clothes. We kids ran along the dikes naked to get home through back yards, only to find relatives with cameras waiting.

I remember large, angled, flat gray rocks in the yard, upon which the wash was scrubbed three hundred years ago, with gulls watching in this small world. A commercial fisherman lived across the street. He would give us kids all the crab legs we could eat. We sat on the grass beside the country road, a feast on this delicacy. A few ducks or chickens meandered down the old pot hole road in front of us. A dog barked at them lazily.

My summer house was light years away from winter reality. What I learned, saw and experienced in and around that island house as a child/teenager always rattled my memories in other homes, places, situations and nations.

Chains with foot irons protruded from a stone wall in an ancient castle in Edinburgh, Scotland, in The Forbidden City, China, at an Inca Temple in Peru and from an attic beam in an unheated room over a kitchen with a pumpkin floor in an island house. It always came with a jolt, freedom is not free!

Once I found am old dockside English Pub in Sydney, Australia with large working walk-in cooking fireplace, painted plank floor boards, wood benches and a narrow mantle for grog mugs. A proportion of Aussies are similar to New Englanders. Honest, straight forward, reliable, cautiously friendly and they always look directly at you when they speak.

Any narrow creek reminds me of skinny dipping on the island, which I repeated in a frigid South American stream, in a tropical jungle to buy land for a banana farm surrounded by vines, flowers, jungle canopy, birds, monkeys and danger.

About three years ago I was in a small bed and breakfast on main street in a village complete with church, fountain, benches, flowers, and bandstand. Our New Hampshire bedroom had a grey painted floor with black and white splatters, six over six windows, and a large fireplace for cooking. Many houses are duplicates of the island house. Since they were seventeen eighteen century homes they are newer and built higher, with fashionable decorative fences, intricate gardens with sundial, gazebo, and fountains. Fancy "his" and "her" outhouses once sat on the rear corners of the property. Some have been converted into tool closets or potting sheds.

Many of these houses were located near a ship warning light. The light house was not visible from March Tavern, but the light was. Fog came with a horn, a taste of salt, damp skin and eeriness.

In the backyard of three different widow's walk houses in various areas of Newburyport, Massachusetts were three engraved tomb stones, each a generation apart.

Captain Rufus Snell	Captain Rufus Snell Jr.	Captain Rufus Snell II
He sailed She waited He returned not She lived not	He went She watched He returned not She lived not	We cannot direct the wind Nor can we adjust the sails We just wait and hope and wither and die

A model constructed by Uncle Bill, of the USS Constitution rested on the living room mantle of the island house. I knew nothing of her history, importance or service to our country. I learned. Eventually I visited this proud ship in Boston Harbor.

At twelve knots our sailboat tacked the huge harbor in Auckland, New Zealand aboard a copy of the America's Cup sailing ship. My memory was on the Merrimack River, Uncle Bill at the wheel of his sailboat with March Tavern in the back ground.

When I was sixteen my uncle's sea captain neighbor invited me to go professional tuna fishing on his ship anchored six blocks from the island house. Dozens of hungry seagulls feasted on entrails and tuna heads. I threw up in the bloody boots. Seagulls had a new perspective.

On July 4th most foreign American Embassys served hot dogs, hamburgers, beans and apple pie to any American. I was in Bogota, Colombia one July 4th. The Ambassador said most large building and homes in Bogota were built after July 4, 1776. I smiled and nodded, March Tavern was 86 years old on July 4th, 1776 and housed braggarts, villains, rich, poor, Indians, murderers, Southerners, slaves, spies, newly-weds, sea captains, youthful innocents and cunning gamblers. Every time I left that house, I was filled with a sadness and even a bit of foreboding that I might never see or smell or feel the comfort of my island house again. I felt the same way when I wandered on some foreign shore.

World War II swallowed me. In a US Navy boot camp, my rifle instructor was amazed at my city boy rifle skills. He inquired how I learned this skill. I told him shooting rats in a marsh dike. He never answered.

As a sailor, I won many poker pots on a heavy cruiser in the North Atlantic. The other sailors didn't know I was an eight year veteran of the March Tavern Poker Club. The island house was what I was fighting for. It was there – solid – I didn't want it hurt or scarred or destroyed. It had sheltered, protected and guarded so many people in so many eras and under so many circumstances. It gave me my childhood teenage life for eight summers, an American point of view and an understanding of humble beginnings.

Years later, when my lifelong friend died at age 30, my Dad was nearly killed in an auto accident and my twenty two year marriage failed, the island house always crept into my mind and I was safe, assured and protected. I could return to that world and feel Laddie's warm body next to mine on the wood kitchen floor, smell the waxed furniture, burning wood and cooking aromas. I was not hurting or alone.

Twenty years ago my special house was sold for physical, economic and practical reasons. My world developed a deep crack. I would never go home again to my special place that gave me strength, warmth, and security. Even today the island house always lounges in a shadow of my mind.

Who would think I could feverishly love bricks, wood, sky, seagulls, wind and smells enough to give me a lump in my throat. My bruised heart was bandaged in keen memories. The house is mine, like my country.

N

Never forget the important little things.

Never stay angry. It's a waste of time.

Never deliberately deceive a person.
The wave will wet your feet.

Never say you will if you don't intend to do it.

Never brag. Let others brag about you.

Never be unkind. It will cost you credibility.

Never is a long time. Use this word infrequently.

Never doubt yourself.

Never wait until tomorrow if today is better.

Never do a little if a lot is required.

Never wait to give love.

NOW

Blowing shaggy silver hair
tight bones
in manure shoe

Mature knees struggle up
between
a trunk and a rock

A quick breeze floats
a delicate memory
through a heartbeat

Communication of mind
and moment
frees me for an instant

In a second pain brings me back
to now

O

Open life slowly.

Opening our eyes each morning is a significant part of our day. It is a perquisite of everything else you want to do in the day.

Our imagination is our wings.

Opening a personal letter is always eventful.

Old age is both wise and comfortable.

An oasis can be found anywhere.

Look carefully at the object of your affections, but be generous.

If something is obscure get a magnifying glass.
Opening any letter is a page of life.

ONE MOMENT

Walking along a Lee road
after
a downpour
a quarter in a puddle
abundance in soft April.

The world not altered
air
not crisper
a rustle of leaves lost no music
life
gave no considering eye.

Yellow buttercups and cowslips
middle May showers
with mumbles of thunder
life gave no coin
no unique moment
one in a pocket

OOZE

A fin swam on his time line
sand and salt ooze between tiny toes
soft ghosts of free yesterday's.

Smudge of oily sand mark a yellow suit
ice cream oozes off his nine year old nose
as he found two perfect sand dollars.

A mark on a faded time line of a drowned friend
ooze streaks on oily pink as he slept.
minnows around aluminum chair legs, small stones.

Time lines grow longer, hover - unexpected curves
the world oozes around his mentally ill mother whose mind froze
but you don't know it as you posse for pictures.

Line of where he had been until one soft goodbye
he learned that ooze of desire is a man's being that never
shows, what was is - until life catches you.

Time line of his father's ever encircling arms
sand and salt ooze follow decade woes
all the way back to the shadow of a fin when he was three
and free.

ONCE DE NOVIEMBRE

The music played day and night for sixty hours as Cartagena, Columbia, South America celebrated the eleventh of November, their independence from Spain, with a monumental celebration. It started slowly Friday morning with several small bands inside the walled city playing quietly, a bit of laugher, singing, and a few small firecrackers.

Half the businesses were open. At noon all closed, placing protection over windows for the frenzy they knew would come. People set up booths for selling booze, ethnic food, gambling, half or full masks and hats. People arrived. The party was on! Crowds, fire crackers, loud music, drinking and dancing in a mad, frantic and crazed atmosphere prevailed.

The next morning, Saturday, the blistering beat of the music was soft! At 7:00 a.m. the plazas were quiet with strains of radio music coming from somewhere and various songs were played simultaneously. Many drunken bodies lay on the ground, stairs, a top the high wall, in corners and on or under tables. Bottles, food, beer cans and whatever littered the plaza and the streets entering it. Sometimes in the day street cleaners did their jobs.

Saturday evening a group of local Americans went back to the finale of this outrageous party. The crowd was enormous. We had costumes similar to the KKK but in solid colors. Hoods could be altered with a scissors for eyes and mouths or a shapes cut out to a fit a mask you made or bought. Stairs or ramps led to the top of the wall surrounding the city. All had access to up or down activities.

Saturday night was a repeat of Friday night but exaggerated. The crowd was untamed, the noise frightening, the constant musical beat wild. We stayed close to the wall or on top of it. The passionate behavior of the revelers was pure animal. Drinking, dancing, kissing, patting, feeling, touching, groping - people disappearing down alleys into deep shadows everywhere. November has excellent weather - no rain, cool breezes and low humidity - a plus for activities.

About eleven p.m. gorgeous fireworks exploded above the enormous Fort San Felipe guarding Cartagena. The Fort enveloped this fiesta of freedom.

Sunday a subdued party with occasional fire crackers continued. Food, gambling, partnered dancing and mild drinking occupied the day. About 4:00 p.m. my friend Jime motioned for me to follow him to a position atop the wall where two streets met forming a "U" shaped wall. An old bull entered this area and the fourth part of this rectangle was closed off. Suddenly poor people swarmed toward the bull carrying machetes, knives, hatchets attacked the bull tearing, ripping and hacking this animal to pieces cruelly, rapidly and quietly. Even the tail, hoofs, penis and testicles were gone. This indelible scene of poverty, hunger and slaughter was primitive and savage.

Soup, stew, chops, tongue, liver and kidney would fill hungry belies tonight.

I looked down over the edge of the wall to the ancient cobbled stone street below as the crowd disappeared. I saw crushed manure mixed with urine and blood.

P

People matter.
People are people. Don't try to change them.
People are not what you expect. Go with the flow.

People are weird.
People are frustrating.
People have flaws, overlook them.

Most people don't change.
People are the best show in town.
Some people say one thing but mean
God knows what.

People can change their lives by changing
their point of view.
Some people are parrots. Pay little mind.
An ounce of principal is worth more
than an ounce of gold.

PERUVIAN JOURNEY
1958

Standing on a street comer in Lima, Peru three streets joined a main road. This worked fine for cars which just merged to get off at the street they wanted. Grandmother stood close to me. There was no corner where cars stopped, and she did not feel fast enough to just dodge cars as the younger people did - and often had trouble.

On this day when traffic was particularly heavy, she hired a taxi to take her across the street.

PERFECTLY POLISHED DAY

April is
spring unfurled
like life

Soft rain
moving streams
night pushed tomorrow

Spring meanders under blue
wait for her
growth is not impulsive

Pick dandelions
and violets
on a soft day

Extraordinary April
moves life
dazzlingly slow

I

Two rows of petals
entangled in a breeze
adventure

Tantalizing buds
April to next day May
Beneath a blue umbrella

Boughs tiny pledge
secret colors
silently

A fleeting glimpse
of lush promise
days snaking past

Each May I find
late tulips, daffodils
a perfectly polished day

2

PEARL

The first time I saw her she was sitting on a restaurant bar stool, her head thrown back laughing at something funny the bartender had said. In one hand a cigarette, in the other a martini. She had on a silver sweater, a long black slit-to- the knee skirt, high heels and a tiny ankle bracelet. I had never met a lady like Pearl.

I leaned against the door jam and watched her for a moment or two. Then she saw me and smiled. A little smile. She dazzled me. We shook hands. That was the beginning. We lived happily ever after. Not quite!

When I met Pearl I was thirty three and divorced for three years. Pearl was thirty eight and divorced one year. We dated. One night I brought her home. She lived with her mom. On the front porch I kissed her.

"Why haven't you made a pass at me?"

"When I make a pass at you you'll want me to make a pass."

That established our relationship. Always tell it like it is.

I pursued her for six months. Carefully but thoroughly. her mother was friendly, polite but felt Pearl could do much better socially and financially if she married a rich Jew. Her two sisters and her brother, the doctor, looked at me as if I were a piece of chewing gum they couldn't get off their shoe.

A school teacher! Not even a supervisor or a principal. One of Pearl's sisters married a liquor store. The other one married a road builder. Big bucks in all directions.

Courting Pearl was not a normal road. She was a professional musician trained at Juilliard School of Music. Pearl had her own five piece band and worked Thursdays, Friday and Saturday from 8 p.m. until 1 a.m. - excellent salary plus tips. She was not beautiful but people never realized that. Her red hair, figure and warm charm were obvious.

On the band stand she wore a knit dress with a metallic weave. Earrings, no necklace bracelet or ring. When that pink spot hit her she was something. When she wore a skirt it was slit to the knee. When she sat at the piano it moved higher. A professional entertainer who knew just how to present the merchandise.

Pearl's voice was not great but good. She could sing a smoky blues song with feeling, understanding, tenderness. Those nimble fingers could play under or over the melody. She did not have to read the music so she looked at the men in the audience. She sang every song to each man in the room. I asked her about that once. She looked me in the eyes.

"That's part of the product. It brings them back."

Jews and Italians are very family oriented. It is a built-in part of their culture. The oldest child was especially close to the Mother. Pearl was it. Jewish Mothers have a fine tuned knack for inflicting guilt feelings on all their children for everything and anything.

We decided to marry. I had a two bedroom apartment in a building my dad owned about ten blocks from Pearl's mom, and we settled comfortably into marriage.

For months I said to Pearl, "Your working is interfering

with our marriage. Our rent is cheap. I have saved money before I met you. Quit."

We argued for a week.

"Mom says we could save a lot of money."

"I'm tired of what mom says, either you quit or I quit."

She quit. For the next twenty-one years we were happy, traveled the world and were good for each other. Mom and I circled each other cautiously.

When I was fifty-nine I suggested to Pearl I would like to retire. Black clouds gathered.

"Work until you are sixty five."

"I don't want to do that. Let's retire to our condo in Florida."

"What about mom?"

"Mom and my brother Bill can visit us for the winter."

I went to Florida alone. No goodbyes. Seven weeks later a letter arrived from a lawyer. I had no idea. Pearl was suing me for a divorce.

I thought we'd cool down in a month or two and talk. It was my pride and her prejudice or was it the opposite? She broke my heart. I don't know what I did to hers.

Do I ever think of her? Sometimes.

Q

Quiet is the soul of your life.

Quills write but why use one when you can use a pen.

Quality cannot be replaced by anything.

Quiet is too good to be true.

Quick is good. Thorough is better.

Quiet surrounds you with calm.

Quality is a distinguishing number – as stamped on silver. Too bad they don't stamp people.

Always look for quality before quantity.

You can't be a quasi friend.

Don't quake from adversity – go forward.

Life is like a patchwork quilt – enjoy the designs.

Never quit. Do you want to establish a pattern?

R

Remember – flowers lean toward the sun.
Evaluate them.

Relax ants, I am leaving.

Rain starting and no umbrella-so?

Revenge is costly. Proceed cautiously.

Rain doesn't fall straight.
Like life, it changes the pattern.

Proper perspective can alter a life.

Never relax your principals.

Don't relish that which you do not know.

Reprimand anyone but a friend.

Don't regret a situation. Change it.

RUM AND COKE

Early each morning I pick up the newspaper in the driveway, sit in my secret place, read the headlines, my horoscope and "Peanuts, Beetle Bailey, and Garfield." You can't worry in a garden.

My flying buttress church birdhouse with steeple, cross, brass bell and two working front doors used to hang in the front yard tree, no tenants, too many cats. I moved the birdhouse to my side yard, twenty five feet high in a tree on a wire. Two birds disputed ownership. The High Episcopal bird won.

There is a birdhouse condominium on different high poles. There is eight inches of aluminum around the top of each pole. A Virginia butterfly house is tall and skinny, a ceramic English thatched roof, three Philadelphia attached row houses, and one Iowa silo. These birds live in high cotton.

I walk through my garden daily and see new things. A spider on a gossamer thread, new growth, a trail of ants, a frog, salamander, garden snake, worm, snail, beetle, lady bug, butterfly, dragon fly and dappled sun on my arm.

I've gotten a few surprises. Huge bee hive developed in a large birdhouse suspended on a wire. The wire rusted, house fell, bees swarmed. So did neighbors.

Garden work goes on and so does the pleasure. Is it worth it? I know it is. You experiment, observe and learn as you go along. Northern spring bulbs - daffodils, tulips, crocus - bloomed only one spring. The next year they had fine growth but no flowers. The ground must freeze for these bulbs to flower again the following spring. There is a wind chime near the large fountain. I glue gunned the top of a large juice can to the stingy wind chime clapper. The chimes ring louder now. My wife gave me a metal table mobile. No wind? A gentle touch with one finger. Birds fly.

Two year old Nolan, my neighbor, comes with his grandmother who lifts him up to push the wind chime clapper. He puts his hands in the low fountain to splash water on a flower pot. He gets wet, the plants not necessarily.

A school for the autistic children is three blocks from my garden. Teachers bring the older children.· I wonder what these children feel and see as they silently look.

I stand in the garden with the sun on my shoulder, not thinking just feeling. It's a part of my next breath. I nurtured, dreamed, sweat, planned, dug, pushed, pulled, prepared beds, planted fertilized and breathed life into this garden. God grew it, but I made it happen.

Quiet is the soul of your life.

"YESTERDAY IS HISTORY, TOMORROW IS A MYSTERY, AND TODAY IS A GIFT: THAT'S WHY THEY CALL IT THE PRESENT."

Eleanor Roosevelt

RAIN
DOESN'T
ALWAYS
FALL
STRAIGHT

S

She wanted more nuts and bolts on the car so the price zoomed.

Sometimes life won't go into words.

Some people settle for the ordinary - if you do the extraordinary, mighty results might be achieved.

Sometimes happiness one finds by luck, chance or in a strange place.

She was not anxious to bloom, she knew she must.

She has something up her sleeve besides her arm.

Some things are best enjoyed from afar.

Spring - a nameless feeling of happiness.

Silence drills a hole into your mind.

Spring rain leaking through a hole in my umbrella like trouble.

Some caterpillars take longer to become a butterfly.

Some people find joy everywhere and leave its glow wherever they go.

SIXTY SECONDS

May breeze
rattled a shutter
above
thorny flowers

Mind meanders
on a beach
salt water whiff
of what

Last night's rain
fell in pelts
puddle
from a drain pipe

Slow drops into ancient fountain
breeze delicately snakes
through silver hair

Spiders dancing on
flimsy lengths of nothing,
abandoned noon shack.

The scarecrows old jacket
torn by winds, bleached and dull,
hopelessly lifeless.

One moment of stillness
that drills into a cliff,
no sound of silence.

Sturdy lonesome shed –
nature silently encroached,
yellow eyes ponder.

First white flakes of nothing
fall into empty grey bowls.
Old dogs settle down.

Sunlight through raindrops
suspended old bark bird house,
cut suet through string.

Grandchildren look hard,
they think my world was ancient.
Perhaps dinosaurs?

April's chilly breeze,
old scarecrow waiving at me.
Should I wave or not?

A string of old socks
some have toe holes, others not –
hang there shivering.

Cat sat watching me
prime the rusty pump handle
we left together.

I wonder just why
the irrigation ditch stops.
Did the shovel die?

In my mind I hear
night shades so still chestnuts
banged the twilight.

Silent snowflakes
each falling spinning dancing
on half finished spring.

Absolutely still
ghost grey dawn sat there brooding,
a flash of hard light.

Gigantic white puffs
suspended real as murky mist
on a blue canvas.

Night cold snap arrived
lilies of the valley slept
surprise blanket – white.

Distant melody,
why does a mind remember
what you can't seem to?

An elegant kite's
lavender tail rises above
those ugly tin shacks.

On a misty day
that butterfly rides upon
the hairs of a bull.

Quiet wind at dusk
lifts one downy white fluff
upon a thistle.

Breeze does not cool you
but moves hungry mosquitoes
searching for an arm.

Niagara Falls fell
stiff drenched smelly rubber,
thundering rumble.

A tiny orphaned child
stumbles carelessly forward
beside a fast stream.

There was that silence.
A bird patting the window
asked attention.

On the streams bottom
the faint shadow of an eel
resting on gray sand.

Unique red water bridge
silently guards her fortress –
oblique authority.

Dawn walks the beach
early footprints disappear,
ripples lap each shape.

Calliope fades,
the soft fall wind still echoes
a melody there.

Hot humid barnyard
fourteen cows tails move the air
swinging at the flies.

From a grey tile roof
those old rats lick beads of dew,
dawn stares.

The forlorn old barn
with its door full of chickens
waiting for the feed.

Silently it falls,
the boy shakes snow from his hair
wetting his cold neck.

Spring gives things away
generously, quietly
but at her own price.

Oh gracious May moon,
deity of that pearl grey sky
toss moonbeams at iris

Today creeps in
on the toes of early gray light
to hide for two blinks.

Brooding nests of dark -
meandering lightening
flicks boney fingers.

Spring gives things away
generously, quietly
but at her own price.

Tomorrow sneaks a peak,
sometime after dawn's eye opens.
What will she see today?

Today creeps in
on the toes of early gray light
to hide for two blinks.

Brooding nests of dark –
meandering lightening
flicks boney fingers.

Those sprinkled snowflakes
as silent as tomorrow
over finished fall.

Rain stops, sun shines free
phenominous refraction –
that rainbow dazzles.

My head could not dodge
the sudden gentle fine rain
nor did I want to.

Sleepy damp stones nestle
too small to be larger rocks
growing up is slow.

Old exhausted cloud
middling lightening flash –
scorched new flowers.

Winter's eve mopes
looking for old friends gone now.
One dimensional.

Acre rows of new hope -
now snow silently descends,
good or now too late.

It won't budge now.
Some headaches never even move.
My eyes closed, I sit.

Search, see, swoop, dive, eat -
where do blind pelicans go
when seeing is done.

When empty clouds paint
a new rainbow before me
I shiver in delight.

The tenants have gone
the grey houses now belong to
nobody but summer winds.

That tolling church bell
either ominous or good
but it does break sleep.

Yellow harvest moon
walking clouds around the lake
tonight, not every night.

Listening in bed
why does the muttering rain
bother me tonight.

So fast that crows flies
his harsh call left an echo
behind in the greens.

Coming from the dell
a parasol has violets
dangling from its points.

T

The sun shines for everybody.

The obvious is difficult to see if you are caught up in the ordinary.

To be happy give your best to whoever, wherever, and however.

The reason to be alive is to live up,
you wouldn't want to live down would you?

The status of love can change in a moment. Be prepared.

The worry storm hid in the memory grove of your mind.

That horn - one long blast, one short.
What's on its mind?

There are no ordinary moments.

The mind's eye is not always right.

The worst thing in the world is not to try.

To plant now, to harvest later.

The great success is to get up after a fall.

The sun will rise. Be prepared to enjoy it.

THAT LONG DAWN

I am wide awake
dark endless hours
I lay here
antenna receiving

My ear hobbles about
one intruding noise or another
chimes from the grandfather's clock
my dad motionless, ice moves in the frig

Endless nothing hours
airplane approach noises
community dumpster emptied
motorcycle rumbles into tomorrow

You remember things to do today
will you remember them at breakfast
things I should have said to my brother
as I held coffee to silent lips

Long nights goodbye
whispering dawn comes
singular washboard of
mountains and valleys

New roads to explore
clean twilight floats
kink in my neck
other nights other ghosts

THEY

I was more eleven
but minus twelve.
The mom I knew changed -
Drifted, withdrew, left.

She sat quietly and wept.
They were going to get her.
A paralyzing fear of what
we never knew.

But they were frightening.
Mom would not be alone ever after.
My Grandma wove a cocoon of love
for Mom and Dad and me.

Many nights four of us cried
ourselves into fitful sleep.
We all felt Mom's pain and ours.
Days, weeks, months, years crept by.

Mom was better. worse, afraid
or between layers of pain.
Years paraded in ghostly memories.
We were each in a private hell.

I

Finally shock treatments worked.
A miracle - severe, bewildering.
Pain blocked in her mind
during a series of procedures.

Mom was a long time
in a strong undertow.
Slowly we swam our
exhausted but never the same.

My friends drifted somewhere.
My family was fractured.
My Mom's mind forever fragile,
I got out almost whole.

I never could put
my family back together.
I was more than eleven
I was one hundred.

2

"THERE IS NO RIGHT WAY TO DO THE WRONG THING."

Anonymous

U

Under stress we see the real person.

Until you sail anything is possible.

Until you accept that nothing is definite you are in trouble.

Until darkness a life time.

Until you realize change is not only inevitable but often good you have a problem.

Until tomorrow, today is all you have.

Until dawn marvelous dreams often happen.

Until you have rain wind and thunder enjoy what you have where you have it.

Under stress move slowly.

Under anxiety stand still.

ULTIMATE

I always wanted to feel
touch
be surrounded
by love
engulfed
enthralled
absolute
an educated heart
calm
assured
warm
complete
I got there
finally
Joan

V

Very late fall grass is what is left of Springs' promise.

Villages without bells. How do they survive?

Victory is not a gift. You must earn it.

Don't vacate a principle

Value yourself.

Never veer from the truth, however painful.

If you don't venture forth nothing will happen.

Be versatile in your mind. But steadfast in your integrity.

VALUE

WHAT YOU LOVE

IT IS

WHAT YOU ARE

W

When we put off living life goes on without us.

When you are deep in winter spring knows it.

When joy comes - take it.

Walking along a rural road, I wondered about the inhabitants of the homestead. All the fences were crooked.

When you slide out your arm from under the covers on a cool night to scratch your nose and slide it back to exactly the same spot.

Why live in a one dimensional world when two is better and three is glorious.

We don't remember days. We remember moments.

Winter is a world of one color which turns to technicolor.

We never recognize the significant moment as it happens.
When life rushes by - walk slower.

WE ARE ALWAYS OURSELVES WHEN WE ARE ALONE

WINTER RAIN PREPARES A SPRING

WET

The storm gathered fast, the scent heavy
wet wind hurled at a yellow slicker
thunder's grumble tumble mumble.

The storm threw sheets of slick cellophane
slaps of rain against chipped steeple
dickered growls of violence.

Electric fingers through cloud's hair
drenched wind slanted water bullets
thunders conflicting echoes roar.

God watched silently
wet jabs smack red wicker
thunder roars as rain softened to flat silver.

Beneath the thunders' last ripple
dribbled a quiet flicker
a beating stillness.

The squall gathered fast but left with muffled quiet
a glistening wet dragon's tail gave one last bicker
defeated it slunk away.

Some storms gather fast
leaving the Amen silence of a vicar -
is rain holy water.

WHIFF OF SALT

I was more than six
not yet seven
summer cot on a wood floor in a tent
lakes and lollipops
learned to swim
before eleven a trailer near a river
row boat, crabs, used sailboat
whiff of salt on a breeze
when you find happiness
put it on
at thirteen Moms mental illness
shock treatments
her Irish wit warmth charm gone
my family
abstract strangers
forever
W.W.II swallowed us, spit me back
alive
whole but different
G.I. bill, college
new me
marriage divorce marriage
would not accept ordinary
worked on three continents
traveled on five
memories
over the rainbow
I never wanted to fly
through one
my my

WE

We always say
I know what I'm going to do
but do we.

We always say
if I do this that will happen -
happenings are slow and dissipate.

We always say
if I have to do it again I will vanish -
no, you get thinner, wiser.

We always say
if I ignore it it will diminish -
why can't we just be - and except.

We always say
I got through yesterday and today -
do tomorrow better.

We know responsibility is thrust upon us.
We do what we must do
because we must.

We know life gives us conflicts
and endurance
for the long haul.

X

Few play the xylophone, fewer a hot one.

Xylophones make beautiful music if you like xylophones.

X-rays can show a broken anything, except a heart.

Y

You're only young once but you can stay immature indefinitely.

If youth is wasted on the young why do we value it?

You never, never, never quit.

You can live nutty occasionally, it brightens up a day.

You need to realize joy, it is a net of love.

You must take Spring when it comes.

You do foolish things occasionally, so do them with enthusiasm.

You know who you are.

Know where you are going.

You can't appreciate happiness without unhappiness.

Your accomplishments require time.

YELLOW

I sat
in a yellow field
my knees a pillow

Upon daffodils -
butterflies
and sunbeams

Such nonchalant gold
waving

Z

Zen is a religion not a philosophy.

The zenith is not always pleasurable.

Don't zig when you should have zagged.

Zealous anything is costly.

A zone is not necessarily where you want to be.

Zeal needs a lot to back it up.

Don't zoom. You miss things.

Don't allow any part of your life to be a zoo.

Put zest in your life whenever possible.

If someone talks about zero be sure to ask zero what?

ZEBRA

He felt
he should hide
from man
behind elephants
luxurious ferns
aspen forest
water fall
grove of bamboo
fog
he was big
fascinatingly decorated
he was himself
as we all are

BIOGRAPHY

Charles Donald Kahrmann

I was born the year Charles Lindburgh flew solo to Paris from New York City, 1927. I am eighty nine years old. I started teaching school in the last two-room pot bellied stove school house in New Jersey in 1951.

I taught elementary education plus fine arts grades kindergarten through twelfth grade and at two universities in New Jersey and one in New York City. I have traveled on four continents and lived on three.

I once had a machete held to my throat in a 1957 meat price riot in Cartagena, Columbia, South America. In 1958 I searched for emeralds at an open pit mine near Bogota, Columbia, South America.

In 1965 I went rafting on the Colorado River wearing a helmet, Mae West knee and elbow pads plus heavy boots. It was incredible. In 1967 I rode on a donkey from the rim of the Grand Canyon to the bottom. It was hot sweaty, scary and gorgeous.

Witnessing dawn at the Inca mystery of Machu Pichu in Lima, Peru in 1969 was dazzling and unbelievable. In 1973 I enjoyed high tea with Ingrid Bergman, in London, between performances of "The Constant Wife". In 1979 I lunched with Joan Fontaine. In 1982 I had a martini with Ray Milland at the Plaza Hotel's Oak Room Bar. His wife was late.

During the summer of 1989 Joan and I floated over the Rio Grande George in a hot of air balloon. The loud dawn silence was pierced by a group of campers who invited us down for breakfast. In 1997 we rode in a hot air balloon over the Li River in China. The mountains looked like loaves of French bread cut in half, and placed on end. Joan saw clouds in the Li River.

In March 2008, we went to Dubai on the Persian Gulf. Dubai is an oil rich piece of desert, about the size of Rhode Island, in the United Arab Emerites. A decade ago it was a pile of sand. It is two hours from Baghdad, close to Iran. Dubai is a new city of skyscrapers - pristine, huge, shiny white towers trimmed in brass and gold! Baghdad by the sea. We were mesmerized.

We have driven across the United States two times. In 2014, we toured our Western National Parks. In September, 2015 we visited Albuquerque, New Mexico for the National Hot Air Balloon Festival. Not over the rainbow, but as close as Joan and I will ever get.

I began to write poetry five years ago and creative writing about nine years ago. Life is curious and serpentine.

TO

ROBERT W. LEREW

WHO

INTRODUCED ME

TO

WRITING

POETRY

GRATEFUL THANKS

www.ingramcontent.com/pod-product-compliance
Lightning Source LLC
Chambersburg PA
CBHW070955040426
42443CB00007B/515
* 9 7 8 1 9 4 2 7 2 8 3 2 0 *